AVROCAR
CANADA'S FLYING SAUCER

AVROCAR

CANADA'S FLYING SAUCER

The Story of
Avro Canada's Secret Projects

Bill Zuk

The BOSTON
MILLS PRESS

Cataloging in Publication Data

Zuk, Bill, 1947-
Avrocar: Canada's flying saucer: the story of Avro Canada's secret projects

Includes bibliographical references and index.
ISBN 1-55046-359-4

1. Research aircraft – Ontario – Malton – History. 2. A. V. Roe Canada Special Projects Group.
I. Title

TL567.R47Z84 2001   629.13'07'2071   2001-930045-X

05 04 03 02 01   1 2 3 4 5

Design by Andrew Smith / PageWave Graphics Inc.
Page layout and composition by Kevin Cockburn / PageWave Graphics Inc.

Printed in Canada

Published in 2001 by Boston Mills Press
132 Main Street, Erin, Ontario, N0B 1T0
Tel 519-833-2407
Fax 519-833-2195
e-mail books@bostonmillspress.com
www.bostonmillspress.com

An affiliate of Stoddart Publishing Co. Limited
895 Don Mills Road
400-2 Park Centre
Toronto, Ontario, Canada, M3C 1W3
Tel 416-445-3333
Fax 416-445-5967
e-mail gdsinc@genpub.com

Distributed in Canada by
General Distribution Services Limited
325 Humber College Boulevard
Toronto, Ontario, M9W 7C3
Orders 1-800-387-0141 Ontario & Quebec
Orders 1-800-387-0172 NW Ontario & other provinces
e-mail cservice@genpub.com

Distributed in the United States by
General Distribution Services Inc.
PMB 128, 4500 Witmer Industrial Estates
Niagara Falls, New York 14305-1386
Toll-free 1-800-805-1083
Toll-free fax 1-800-481-6207
e-mail gdsinc@genpub.com
www.genpub.com

THE CANADA COUNCIL | LE CONSEIL DES ARTS
FOR THE ARTS | DU CANADA
SINCE 1957 | DEPUIS 1957

We acknowledge for their financial support of our publishing program the Canada Council, the Ontario Arts Council,
and the Government of Canada through the Book Publishing Industry Development Program (BPIDP).

CONTENTS

FOREWORD

I WAS RESEARCHING information on hypersonic air vehicles some years ago when I tripped over the remarkable story of the Kingfish. Kingfish had been proposed by General Dynamics Convair against a bid from Lockheed as a replacement for the CIA's Lockheed U-2 spyplane. Its performance data were staggering. With its two-man crew, Kingfish would have cruised the stratosphere at 125,000 feet at Mach 6 for thousands of miles without refuelling. Such performance is barely conceivable today. But the specification for Kingfish was drawn up in 1958. It was tantalizing because I had never even heard of it, nor had people who prided themselves on the aeronautical history of the period.

Why is Kingfish relevant to this fascinating history of Canada's flying saucer projects by Bill Zuk? For a number of reasons. When I asked for details from the chief designer of Convair, who was then eighty years old, he was reluctant to furnish them, saying that forty years on the matter were still very sensitive. When I went to the CIA and asked for records that might shed further light on the story, I was told that they were classified. This was remarkable for a project that didn't actually go anywhere—if officialdom is to be believed. For the record, it was Lockheed that went on to win the CIA contract with a design called the A-12. This later became the U.S. Air Force's SR-71, at Mach 3, the fastest jet aircraft ever built.

That an aircraft like Kingfish could go undocumented in open-source literature for so long is a testimony to the secrecy that prevailed at the end of the 1950s—a culture that is still prevalent, of course, within today's aerospace and defence industry. The shame of it is that remarkable projects, inspired by remarkable people, run the risk of remaining forever obscure as documentation gets shredded and designers take the details to their graves. National security is one thing, but after the passage of so many years, it ceases to be relevant and instead borders on the criminal. These stories need to be told or they will be lost for all time.

Bill Zuk's book on Canada's flying saucers is not simply the history of an extraordinary program, but of a company, Avro Canada, and a national aerospace industry in transition. With a number of cutting-edge projects on the go in the late 1950s, not the least of which was the Avro Arrow, Canada's aerospace industry looked set for a glittering future. But within a few short years, the dream was shattered, and it would be decades before Canadian aviation would again be able to hold its head high. Now, it is once more among the most successful and productive industries in the world.

Many aviation enthusiasts know of the story of the Avrocar, but until now, few people—quite possibly only those who were directly involved in it—have known the story of what went on behind it, of Project Y / Silverbug and its various iterations and the Avro Special Projects Group. With this book, the obfuscation that had clouded the activities of the group at this time has been removed. Reading it, I felt the same fascination for the past that I experienced on the trail of the Kingfish.

The only mysteries to my mind are why the history of Canada's secret saucer projects remained buried for so long, and whether America deliberately brought about their downfall. Was it a willful act of sabotage or was it negligence on all sides that killed them? And was it the demands of secrecy or simply embarrassment over something that went wrong that kept insiders from talking?

Read this illuminating book and decide for yourselves.

Nick Cook, Aviation Editor,
Jane's Defence Weekly, London, June 2000

FOREWORD 2

OVER THE YEARS, there have been many reports from around the world of flying saucers or unidentified flying objects (UFOs) in the sky. The vast majority of these reports have explanations, although not always acceptable to the lay person. And whenever there is mention of flying saucers, there seem to be several varying opinions. First, there are those who look at the subject as utter nonsense and totally beyond the realm of possibility in the past, present and future. Another group is one that seems sure we are not alone on planet Earth and that we have been visited from time to time by little green men or other strange creatures from outer space. Many of this latter group imply that local authorities and government bodies are all involved to varying degrees in a gigantic cover-up. And it would seem that there is a final, far larger group that keeps an open mind and tends to suspect that where there is smoke, there is at least the possibility of a little fire.

Rapid advances in aviation, science and related technologies during the Second World War and in the years since have given rise to many rumours, half-truths and at least some facts about flying saucers, many of which have been exploited to the fullest in films and books on the subject. However, in Canada during the years 1952–1962, a true flying-saucer project was developed by the Special Projects Group led by Chief Designer John Frost, at Avro Canada in Malton, Ontario.

John Frost had originally arrived in Canada from the United Kingdom to work on the design of the Avro Canada all-weather interceptor, the CF-100. But when the aircraft began production, Frost became somewhat redundant. It is not hard to visualize that with all the aviation talent assembled around him at Malton, he may have thought it was a good time to investigate some of the ideas that he had been thinking about for the past while, in relation to aircraft with vertical takeoff and landing (VTOL) capabilities. Looking over the activities he was undertaking during this period, one quickly realizes that John was not your run-of-the-mill aeronautical designer but rather an original thinker who was likely to charge off in new directions, seemingly to try to determine where a strange road might lead. This trait could and did lead to some quite uncomplimentary remarks being made about Frost and his radical ideas, by other, more conventional designers and engineers within Avro, both in Canada and the United Kingdom.

One must remember that at this time, Avro Canada was deeply involved with the Canadian government and the Royal Canadian Air Force (RCAF) in the design of a replacement for the CF-100. This was, of course, the CF-105 Avro Arrow program, with a design team led by Jim Floyd. The totally Canadian-designed Arrow, with its guidance system, weapon systems and Orenda Iroquois jet engine, was staggering in its demand for funding, even in 1952. Under these conditions, it is not difficult to see the opposition in Avro Canada to Canadian government funds being diverted to the high-risk projects that John Frost was advocating. As it worked out, it was soon after his leaving the CF-100 design team that Frost presented his ideas to Avro management at Malton, and the Special Projects Group was formed. The following is an attempt to document in detail the activities of the Special Projects Group under the leadership of J. C. M. Frost.

Les Wilkinson, 1980

CHAPTER ONE

THE STORY BEGINS

I DIDN'T KNOW much about the story of Avro Canada's flying saucer projects, other than what I had read as a schoolboy growing up in the 1950s. What had fascinated me about Avro Canada was the story of the legendary Avro Arrow, that hallowed icon of Canada's aviation past and could-have-been future. As an air cadet, I had my eyes on a career flying military planes in the Royal Canadian Air Force, but I had despaired, as a youth, the decision to cancel the superlative interceptor.

With the loss of the Arrow came disillusionment, maybe as much as that I felt when I learned later, at the age of sixteen, that my eyes weren't "good enough," and I would need glasses. Almost as a last resort, I applied for an Air Cadet flying scholarship and trained strenuously with a school copy of Shakespeare's *Hamlet*, squinting at the footnotes till I could read the page at arm's length. I somehow got through the eye exam, but even throughout the training I received that summer, after I soloed my plane, I surreptitiously snuck a pair of new eyeglasses into the cockpit with me.

I gave up my dream of flying and went to university and a career in teaching. But it all came back in 1997 when the CBC film *The Arrow* arrived in Winnipeg. After reading a newspaper article on the making of the movie, on an impulse, I went down to the hangar where the film crew was constructing a full-scale model replica of the Avro Arrow. Talking my way in, I went on to explain to a PR type that I knew the story about the aircraft and asked if they would mind if I chronicled the making of the film for publication. To my surprise, he agreed and gave me full access to the filming locations. I eventually wrote a number of articles and began to learn more about the background of A. V. Roe Canada.

CF-105 Avro Arrow Mk. 1, RL-201 piloted by Janusz Zurakowski in a climb.

Hugh Mackechnie / c. 1958 / 79262 Avro Aircraft Ltd.

Later that year, while in Toronto on a trip to see my youngest son, I looked up Les Wilkinson, one of the authors of *Arrow*, the heralded book on the CF-105 Avro Arrow. I met with him essentially to have him read the manuscript of one of my new projects, but found that an elderly but energetic Wilkinson had something very different in mind for me. He casually looked over my work and then began to tell me a story about Avro Canada and a man he called a visionary genius—John Frost.

The year was 1954. It was the beginning of an incredible decade of opportunity and dreams, inventions and discoveries. Around the world, news headlines proclaimed: "U.S. Supreme Court Rules that Segregation by Color in Public Schools is a Violation of Constitution, St. Lawrence Seaway Project Approved by Eisenhower, Nobel Prize for

Literature: Ernest Hemingway for 'Old Man and the Sea,' Hydrogen Bomb Tested at Bikini, Jonas E. Salk Starts Inoculating Schoolchildren for Polio," and "29 Million U.S. Homes Have Television."

Meanwhile, in Canada, a little-known event was taking place on a dark September evening in Toronto, Ontario. A group of four Avro Canada engineers hovered around the hood of a black Pontiac sedan. The tall, gangly leader of the group made some final adjustments to an apparatus that protruded from the hood and was fixed to the windshield and roof. Sitting precariously out in front of the car was a metal disc. As they all clambered into the car, the driver fired up the engine and swung out onto a narrow dirt road that circled the runway at Malton airport. As the driver, T. Desmond "Des" Earl pushed the car faster, he began calling out the speed. "Jack" Frost kept his eye on the model balancing on the long boom in front, then he got out on the running board of the car and stared into the darkness to make out the vibrating silver disc. "I actually got it up to eighty-five miles an hour," Earl related in a televised interview in 1993.

The car slowed and both of them began laughing at the sheer silliness of the scene. "Not very scientific," Des recalled with a laugh, years later. "There was a tendency to do a quick and dirty test on something that is a new, good idea, to know whether you want to go that way and do more elaborate

L–R, Ernest Ball, Arnold Rose, John Frost and Des Earl driving a 1952 Pontiac up to its top speed to evaluate the flight characteristics of a flying-disc model. c.1953 / via Des Earl

tests later, more rigorous ones." The test was another example of John Frost's unconventional way of thinking. Bill Lamar, an American scientist who worked closely with Frost, once described him as "a genius...here was a guy if you asked a question, the next day would have the answer flying in the lab."

This episode is part of the story of Canada's flying saucer and of the engineers and technicians of A. V. Roe Canada—a remarkable group of people who dreamed the impossible and nearly made it happen.

CHAPTER TWO

A. V. ROE CANADA

THE BIRTH OF A. V. ROE CANADA

In 1946, after six years of war, Canada was about to make a fundamental change in its place in the world. Immediately following the end of the Second World War, Canadians were in a position to leave forever an agrarian economy and enter one based on industrialism.

During the course of the war, plants and factories vital to the war effort had sprung up all over the country. These industries were primarily engaged in munitions and armament production, which included tanks, warships and aircraft. One of the most important aviation companies was Victory Aircraft at Malton, Ontario, in the former National Steel Car buildings, located northwest of Toronto, which were owned by the federal government. Today, the main buildings of the former Victory plant are part of the Boeing Aircraft plant in the Lester B. Pearson International Airport complex in Toronto.

Victory had been the largest aviation company in Canada and had turned out a significant number of aircraft for the Royal Air Force (RAF) and the Royal Canadian Air Force (RCAF) for use in the European theatre of operations. Its production included the Avro Anson, a twin-engined bomber/trainer, and the famous four-engined Avro Lancaster bomber that was the backbone of the Allied night assault in Europe. Eventually, Victory produced 422 Avro Lancasters, 78 Avro Ansons, 5 Westland Lysanders, 8 Avro Lancaster XPP transports (similar to the Lancastrian), one Avro York transport and one Avro Lincoln bomber.

Roy Dobson (later Sir Roy Dobson), the enterprising managing director of the A. V. Roe Company (United Kingdom), part of the Hawker-Siddeley Group of companies, had visited the Victory Aircraft "branch plant" in 1942 and 1943. He had been highly impressed with the Lancaster production team. Following the cessation of hostilities, Dobson made arrangements for the British Hawker-Siddeley Group to purchase the company and its sprawling plant near the Toronto airport. On November 2, 1945, an agreement

A. V. ROE CANADA TIMELINE

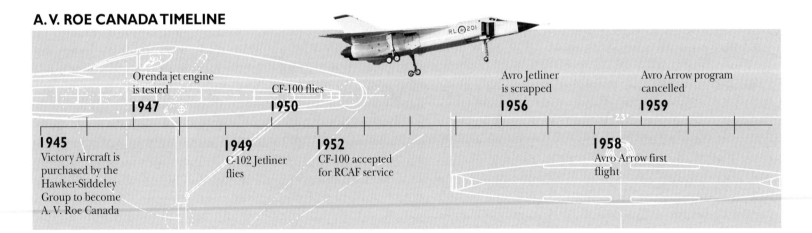

Orenda jet engine is tested
1947

CF-100 flies
1950

Avro Jetliner is scrapped
1956

Avro Arrow program cancelled
1959

1945
Victory Aircraft is purchased by the Hawker-Siddeley Group to become A. V. Roe Canada

1949
C-102 Jetliner flies

1952
CF-100 accepted for RCAF service

1958
Avro Arrow first flight

general manager of the new company. Mr. Dobson and the A. V. Roe Canada management made great plans for the company and for the country.

THE A. V. ROE CANADA DESIGN TEAM

Smye, together with a select group of English designers, including Joe Lindsay (Armstrong-Siddeley Gas Turbines), W. G. Carter (Gloster Aircraft), W. Downing (also from Glosters) and S. D. (Stu) Davies (A. V. Roe), planned a number of projects. In a series of meetings in Canada late in 1946, their proposals were for the new company to undertake the design of a jet engine, jet fighter and jet airliner.

Avro Canada Plant. The Orenda Division is at the top right. Special Projects Group was headquartered there.   c. 1956 / via Les Wilkinson

Inset: Avro Aircraft plant at a shift change, September 1949.   1949 / Gilbert A. Milne

was signed with the Liberal government to turn over the facilities to form A. V. Roe Canada Limited. It was thought to be a very favourable arrangement for the British concern, as Dobson acquired an impressive production facility for a capital stock investment of $2.5 million Canadian.

However, the formidable minister for munitions and supply in Canada's government, C. D. (Clarence Decatur) Howe, made sure the provisions of the agreement included specifications that the new company would be involved in design and development and that it would be essentially a Canadian concern with Canadian management. Although Dobson was its first president, he appointed

Canadians such as J. P. Bickell, formerly president of Victory Aircraft, as chairman of the board and Walter Deisher from Fleet Aircraft in Fort Erie, Ontario, the first vice-president and general manager.

The first employee of A. V. Roe Canada was another Canadian, Fred Smye, the former assistant general manager of Federal Aircraft in Montreal, who took on the role of

A. V. Roe Canada assembled a very talented design team. Although many key personnel, such as Jack Millie, came from the former Victory Company, the remainder of the team, with the exception of Canadian James A. Chamberlin (from Noorduyn Aircraft), who joined the team as the chief aerodynamicist, was made up of mainly English engineers. Edgar Atkin was chief engineer. Bob Lindley, an engineer, and Jim Floyd, a designer, came from the chief home company, A. V. Roe, in Manchester, England. John Frost came later from de Havilland (United Kingdom) to complete the exceptional group.

THE JETLINER

Their first project was a jet transport aircraft designed with one customer in mind—Trans-Canada Air Lines (now Air Canada). The Avro Canada C-102 Jetliner was originally designed in England by James C. Floyd, but Floyd and the design were then transferred to the fledgling Canadian company. After some initial difficulties, which were to be expected when breaking new technological barriers, the aircraft had its first flight on August 10, 1949. It was flown by Jim Orrell, chief test pilot for Avro (United Kingdom), only thirteen days after the British flew their Comet jet airliner.

The Avro Canada C-102 Jetliner was the first jet transport flying in North America, making the first international jet transport flight from Toronto to New York in April 1950. The Jetliner, flown mainly by Avro Canada's chief test pilot, Don Rogers, aroused much interest in the United States and was one of the outstanding aeronautical achievements of its day—a jet airliner that could fly at speeds exceeding 800 kilometres per hour (500 m.p.h.). Even the American press was quoted in Jim Floyd's book, *The Avro Canada C102 Jetliner*, as saying that this aircraft proved that "Uncle Sam has no monopoly on brains." It would be seven years before the Americans flew a jet transport.

The company had a success, or thought they had. But unfortunately, the Avro Jetliner never saw production. Trans-Canada Air Lines, Canada's premier airline, had been interested in the Jetliner during its design

August 10, 1949: Avro C-102 Jetliner on its first test flight, flown by Jim Orrell, chief test pilot for Avro (U.K.), only thirteen days after the British flew their Comet jet airliner. 1949 / Gilbert A. Milne

phase but lost interest even before the first flight, as it was clear that the jet could not compete on longer, more profitable routes. In the Cold War atmosphere of the early 1950s, C. D. Howe, then the minister of reconstruction in Canada's government, insisted that the Avro company concentrate on their other jet program, the CF-100 fighter. That decision was to have long-lasting effects on the future of the company.

Even the RCAF, the first air force to operate jet transports, ordered two de Havilland Comets in November 1951. After no sales were generated in foreign markets (although Howard Hughes had evaluated the Jetliner extensively for TWA), the Avro Canada Jetliner was sold for scrap in 1956. Today, only the nose section and one engine survive in the National Aviation Museum at Rockcliffe, Ottawa, Ontario. One other engine was in the private collection of the late Bob Johnson, one of the earlier Victory Aircraft and A. V. Roe Canada employees at the Malton complex.

THE ORENDA

In the late 1930s, the invention of the jet engine by Frank Whittle of Great Britain and Germany's Hans von Ohain created a revolutionary new kind of aircraft propulsion system. The jet engine had seen operational use in a number of wartime fighters and bombers, including the Messerschmitt Me-262, the Heinkel He-163, the Arado 234 from Germany, the American Lockheed F-80 and the British Gloster Meteor. The speeds of these aircraft were remarkable, as they leaped ahead of conventional piston-engined fighters into the range of 800–900 kilometres per hour (500–600 m.p.h.).

In the postwar period, as noted by Wilfrid Eggleston in *Canada at Work*, the jet engine "particularly interested Canada...because early reports asserted that the new engine would be light and powerful, simple in principle, possibly easy to design, and probably not too difficult to manufacture." By 1942, Canada had already investigated the technical difficulties

in the jet engine, and the National Research Council (NRC) had built a cold-weather experimental station in Winnipeg to test engines at freezing and below-freezing temperatures. A long-term jet-engine development plan by the Canadian government included the establishment of a Crown corporation—Turbo Research Limited— in 1944.

The new company took over the NRC's research on cold-weather operation and began recruiting and training a research and development team. Members of this team, "the one hundred men," were sent to Britain for additional training in advanced jet-engine techniques. Turbo Research and the RCAF drew up a provisional specification for an aircraft jet engine that year, and by war's end, research into jet engines led to an experimental engine known as the Chinook.

When Roy Dobson acquired the former Victory Aircraft plant in 1945, there was also great interest in the existing research and development work carried out on jet engines

Orenda test rig to evaluate the turborotor outside the Schaeffer building. Exhaust gases from an Orenda engine were diverted to a Y-shaped duct. Initial tests of the turborotor took place with this rig.

c. 1958 / via Les Wilkinson

in Canada, and by arrangement with the Canadian government, Turbo Research was part of the deal. Existing staff and equipment were transferred to the Malton site in an expanded facility across from the main A. V. Roe Canada plant. This new division of A. V. Roe Canada, renamed the Gas Turbine Division, was under the direction of P. B. Dillworth as manager and chief engineer.

The Chinook engine design continued throughout 1946 as a means to confirm design and development objectives, as well as to help set up production standards for manufacturing jet engines. By March 1948, the Chinook had its first operational test, with an initial thrust of 1,315 kilograms (2,900 lbs.). A test facility near Parry Sound—the Nobel Test Establishment (a former wartime explosives plant)—provided the basis of a test plant for compressors, combustion chambers and turbines. Much of the testing equipment already designed by Turbo Research was manufactured in the A. V. Roe shops.

By April 1947, the engine division had its first contract for the TR-5 Orenda Mark 1 jet engine, with Chief Designer Winnett Boyd heading up the project. He had created a ten-stage axial compressor with six combustion chambers and a single-stage turbine, and the initial test results, on February 10, 1949, had shown an outstanding 2,830-kilogram (6,250 lb.) thrust. (The contemporary-production Rolls-Royce Nene had a 2,268-kilogram [5,000 lb.] thrust, while the General Electric J-47 had 2,680-kilogram [5,910 lb.] thrust.)

An Avro Lancaster (FM209) was converted into a flying test bed for the Orenda jet engine. Two jet engines replaced the outboard Merlin piston engines in this test aircraft, and after successful flight testing in 1950, another conversion was undertaken that had long-term results. The F-86 Sabre had been chosen as the RCAF's day fighter, to be built under licence by Canadair Limited of Cartierville, Quebec. The decision to power the Sabre with the Orenda would ensure continuous supply but was also a good political decision, creating a more "Canadian" aircraft. The Orenda-powered Sabre was a success, and after the prototype was flown at the North American plant in California, the remainder of the Canadair Sabre production line used various versions of the Orenda series. The Mark 2 Orenda powered the first flight of the CF-100 Mk. 2 in 1951, and from then on, the Orenda was also the engine used in the Avro CF-100 series.

THE CF-100 CANUCK

Avro Canada's main jet programs in the 1950s were based on the CF-100 Canuck, the first military jet aircraft wholly designed and built in Canada. The name, Canuck, was considered inappropriate at the time for a fighter, and unofficially, pilots called it the "Clunk" and the "Lead Sled." Millie and Chamberlin had been involved in its initial design, before Frost came on as project designer. He would later leave the team to head up a special projects section in 1952.

Avro CF-100 Mk. 4B Canucks from 428 Squadron.

c. late 1950s / Hugh Mackechnie

Avro CF-100 18105, flown by Avro test pilot Peter Cope in a JATO (jet-assist takeoff).

1952 / Verne Morse

Below: Avro CF100s in formation over a northern NORAD station. c. late 1950s / National Archives

After four years of development, the Avro Canada CF-100 first flew in January 1950. The CF-100 Canuck was a long-range, all-weather interceptor equipped with two Avro Canada designed and built Orenda engines. It was destined to be the only Avro Canada aircraft to go into full production, and to enter into active service. The CF-100 Canuck became operational in April 1953 and served for ten years as a front-line fighter in NORAD and NATO squadrons. Eventually, 692 were built, with 53 sold to Belgium.

While the CF-100 was not as fast as contemporary fighters such as the North American F-86 Sabre, its good climb rate, excellent

Avro CF-100 Mk. 4B Canucks from 428 Squadron.

c. late 1950s / Hugh Mackechnie

GROWTH AND EXPANSION

In 1951, in the midst of teething development problems in the CF-100 program, A. V. Roe Canada Limited acquired a new and dynamic Canadian CEO. Dobson, now chairman of the Hawker-Siddeley Group, appointed Crawford Gordon Jr. to oversee the troubled operation as its president.

Gordon followed the suggestion of Stuart Davies in the restructuring of the design office: Jim Floyd became chief engineer early in 1952, replacing Atkin and assuming responsibility for what Jim Floyd termed "the executive management of the aircraft engineering division." Shortly after these changes, Gordon divided the operation into two separate organizations—the Aircraft Division, with Smye as general manager, and the Gas Turbine Division, with Tom McCrae as general manager.

A. V. Roe Canada began to diversify, as the Hawker-Siddeley Group invested more in its Canadian subsidiary. By 1954, the company was undergoing an industrial expansion, diversifying into shipping, steel products, truck and bus transportation, iron and coal mining, railway rolling stock, computers and electronics. On July 29, 1954, the Aircraft Division was incorporated as Avro Aircraft Limited and was commonly known as Avro Canada. The Gas Turbine Division became Orenda Engines Limited. The non-aviation subsidiary was Canadian Steel Improvement Limited, and was later joined by Dosco, the Dominion Steel and Coal Corporation, in 1958.

radar, twin-engined reliability and all-weather capability made it suitable for defence in the extreme conditions of the Canadian North, and later in NATO service in Europe. Company test pilot Janusz Zurakowski also dove the CF-100 through the sound barrier—making it one of the first straight-winged jet aircraft to accomplish this feat.

After a long service career, the CAF finally retired the Canuck in 1981. Today, two Avro CF-100 Canucks are preserved in Canada's National Aviation Museum in Ottawa, one at the Calgary Aerospace Museum, one at the Western Canada Aviation Museum and others in parks and bases across Canada, including Mountainview, Ontario, and the Air Heritage Park at the Air Command Headquarters in Winnipeg.

But even before the CF-100 went into service, the RCAF was looking for a replacement interceptor, expecting to need one nine or ten years down the road. After an exhaustive world search for an aircraft to meet the Air Force specifications, Avro Canada was given the go-ahead on their design proposal—the CF-105, later called the Avro Arrow.

THE CF-105 ARROW

In the 1950s, Canadian and American air-defence organizations were integrated under the NORAD Agreement, and a continental radar defence network was completed. The Canadians and Americans had foreseen the requirement for an interceptor of advanced design that could effectively exploit the advantages of this system. Encouraged by A. V. Roe's success in developing the Avro CF-100 Canuck, and recognizing the need for an aircraft to counter the threat of Soviet bombers over the demanding Canadian North, the new Avro design was the company's most complex and sophisticated project.

By December 1953, enthusiastic RCAF officers, defence scientists and defence-industry officials had persuaded the Liberal government to authorize two prototype airframes of an advanced supersonic interceptor. It was anticipated that a production run of up to 600 aircraft costing $2 million (Canadian) apiece was needed, and the supersonic jet interceptor was scheduled to be ready for use by the RCAF in late 1961. The Avro design, later designated Project Number CF-105, was designed to RCAF specifications in 1953, and called for a twin-engine, two-seat interceptor, capable of protecting the Arctic frontier of Canada.

CF-105 Avro Arrow Mk. 1 RL-201 piloted by Janusz Zurakowski, in a classic photo pass over Niagara Falls. c. 1958 / Hugh Mackechnie

The CF-105 was extraordinary in its execution; unlike its subsonic predecessor, the CF-100, the new design, officially designated the Arrow, represented an advanced technological achievement. The fully developed CF-105 Arrow Mk. 2 would have been capable of Mach 2.5 speeds—amazing for 1959!

The design originated from the innovative research and design programs carried out by Avro in the 1940s. The sleek, delta-wing design with high-mounted wing, powered by

Canadian-designed Iroquois engines with 11,839-kilogram (26,100 lb.) thrust in afterburning mode, far exceeded the design specifications. Early proposals, project studies and tests, which later resulted in the basic CF-105 design, were largely the responsibility of the Preliminary Design Office, where Ken Barns was an important member of the team. The office was run by Chamberlin under Floyd, chief engineer and later vice-president of engineering. A very tight schedule was in place from the time of initial design to delivery to the RCAF for squadron use. The first wind-tunnel tests were made in September 1953, and preliminary design of the Arrow was completed by the summer of 1954. An innovative approach was undertaken by the Avro Company to establish production tooling from the outset, resulting in the first Arrow reaching completion status on October 4, 1957.

RL-201 was the first of five Arrow Mk. 1 aircraft that would fly as prototypes for the series. Carrying Pratt and Whitney J-75 engines in the interim, the initial production batch was still a fascinating hint of the future. Using a complex "fly-by-wire" control, an advanced weapons system and remote ground-controlled operation, the Arrow was, arguably, the most advanced fighter aircraft of its day in the western world. A very sophisticated weapons system, designated the Astra I, which consisted of an integrated airborne system for electronic weapons navigation and communications, was incorporated into the Arrow. It provided automatic flight control, airborne radar, telecommunications and navigation, as well as special instrumentation and pilot displays, and could operate in either fully automatic, semiautomatic, or manual environments. This system was the prime responsibility of Radio Corporation of America, in association with the Aeronautical Division of Minneapolis-Honeywell. The Canadian firms of RCA Victor Company of Canada, Honeywell Controls Limited, and Computing Devices of Canada, received subcontracts for engineering services.

During the design phase, Avro Canada undertook the expensive development of the Arrow's engine, and fire-control and missile systems, based on the Douglas Sparrow Mk. 2, with estimated costs rising to $12.5 million per aircraft. Test flights indicated that, with the definitive engines, the plane could well be the world's fastest and most advanced interceptor. However, doubts in the military and the government over the

Avro Arrow CF-105 Mk. 2 RL-206 nose section and starboard main undercarriage unit on display at the Museum of Science and Technology, Ottawa. Today this section and related undercarriage and wind panels are part of the National Aeronautical Collection of the National Aviation Museum in Ottawa. c. 1975 / CAF

Avro Arrow CF-105 Mk. 2 RL-206 nose section and nose wheel on display at the National Aviation Museum in Ottawa. This section and related undercarriage and wing panels are part of the museum collection. The engine at right is an Orenda Iroquois that would have powered the Mk. 2 series. c. 1996 / Bill Zuk

role of the Arrow mounted, and the government reduced its order to one hundred aircraft, while unit costs rose.

The first engine running of the Arrow with a Pratt and Whitney J-75 engine took place on December 4, 1957, and Janusz Zurakowski, chief development test pilot of Avro Canada, began taxi tests on Christmas Eve, 1957. On the first test flight of the Arrow on March 25, 1958, systems were checked and instrument readings noted. The soft-spoken Zurakowski remembers that he said simply, "It handled very nicely."

The first two flights of the Avro Arrow were for pilot familiarization. Then the aircraft went supersonic (Mach 1.4) on the third flight on April 3, 1958, at a height of 12,000 metres (39,000 ft.). But the true potential of the Avro Arrow was realized on the seventh flight of RL-201 on August 23, 1958, when Zurakowski exceeded 1,600 kilometres per hour (994 m.p.h.) at an altitude of 15,240 metres (50,000 ft.) in a climb, while still accelerating. Zurakowski also flew the second prototype on August 1, 1958, and while on his first flight in the third prototype on September 22, 1958, he exceeded the speed of sound!

In the end, he made twenty-two flights in the Arrow RL-201, RL-202 and RL-203, for a total of twenty-three hours, forty-five minutes. Zurakowski flew the Arrow on all of its initial flights, until October 1, 1958, when he retired as chief development test pilot for Avro Canada. "I test flew the Arrow Mark 1 on twenty-two flights, including the first flight. My highest speed was Mach 1.89, achieved on the twentieth flight. My deputy test pilot, 'Spud' Potocki, reached Mach 1.98 on flight number forty-four. I think the aircraft could have reached Mach 2.1 or 2.2 with the J-75 at forty to fifty thousand feet. We expected to do Mach 2.5 with the Orenda Iroquois."

Potocki made the first flight in Arrow RL-204 on November 27, 1958, and the first and only flight in Arrow RL-205 on January 11, 1959. As one of the few test plots left at Avro Canada after February 1959, Potocki also undertook the test program of the VZ-9-AV Avrocar.

THE FLYING SAUCER PROJECTS

The Avro Arrow was not the only innovative design project underway by the company. A. V. Roe Canada had also become involved in an incredible number of progressive designs that pushed the envelope in many directions; it was estimated that at that time 70 percent of Canada's research and development ventures were being carried out by the company. Most of these "paper projects" remained in the conceptual stage, but they were a unique vision of the future. However, in the recesses of the factory, another aircraft project was beginning to come alive under the direction of John Frost.

Project Y mockup under construction.

c. 1953 / Avro Aircraft Ltd.

The concept of the ground cushion was one that Frost had envisioned as being the basis for a vehicle that could have VTOL (vertical takeoff and landing) capabilities and could still operate as an aircraft. His ideas revolved around a disc or saucer shape—a "flying saucer."

By July 1952, the concept was code named Project Y, and the design group had not only completed a number of reports but had also constructed a wooden mockup. After a meeting in England with members of the design group and Frost, Sir Roy Dobson was enthusiastic in his support. The project then gained both momentum and controversy.

At Avro Canada, other designers, including Chamberlin and Floyd, were less than enthusiastic. There was also pressure from the Canadian government through Howe's office to concentrate on only the successful CF-100 and Orenda programs. But Frost continued to lobby for the project, now called the Y-2, and achieved an extraordinary breakthrough by demonstrating the project to the United States Air Force. With funding from the Americans, Frost could proceed with his design even without Avro Canada's support.

From 1955 to 1959, the design team concentrated on the VTOL program, which spawned the VZ-9-AV Avrocar.

POLITICS

Other events were soon to overtake A. V. Roe Canada. After years of ruling Liberal governments, the newly elected Progressive Conservative government of the Right Honourable John G. Diefenbaker reviewed the government's current commitments. Diefenbaker considered the Avro Arrow program the previous Liberal government's pet project. On September 23, 1958, the prime minister made a five-page announcement to the press.

He said, in part, that in recent weeks the Canadian air defence program had been fully reviewed by the government. The U.S.S.R.'s launch of an intercontinental ballistic missile was raising doubts about the priority of the Soviet bomber threat. It believed, however, that it would be unwise to abruptly discontinue the development of the Arrow and its engine because of the effects upon the Canadian aviation industry. Therefore, the government decided that the development program for the Arrow aircraft and the Iroquois engine should be continued until March 1959, when the situation would be reviewed again.

Considering the rapid development taking place during the previous year in missiles for both offence and defence, the Diefenbaker government decided that it would be clearly unwise to continue the costly and protracted development of the Avro CF-105 Arrow. So the Astra flight and fire-control system for the CF-105 and the Sparrow II air-to-air missile contracts were terminated immediately. However, A. V. Roe Canada was unaware that the Canadian government had already made another momentous decision.

BLACK FRIDAY

In the meantime, modifications to the CF-105 would be made during its development to permit the use of the Hughes fire-control-and-weapon system already in production for U.S. interceptors. The Canadian government renewed its efforts to sell the aircraft to the United States, at the same time that the U.S. was promoting the Boeing IM-99 Bomarc anti-aircraft missile. Bomarc missiles had been proposed by the Diefenbaker cabinet as an adequate deterrent, and the government had decided to introduce the Bomarc into Canada's air defence system. But supporters of the CF-105 Avro Arrow greatly resented the promotion of the cost-effective (but highly flawed) Bomarc.

As Gordon launched a last-ditch effort to keep the Arrow project going, it was clear there was considerable resistance in the Diefenbaker government to continuing with the costly development of the Arrow. More importantly, the Canadian chiefs of staff had already effectively doomed the Arrow program with a negative review of its costs and repercussions on future equipment procurement for other military needs.

After efforts at selling the Arrow again failed, Prime Minister Diefenbaker officially cancelled the Avro Arrow program on February 20, 1959 (known as "Black Friday" at Avro). The announcement in the House of Commons, as reported in *Hansard*, stated, "The government has carefully examined and reexamined the probable need for the Arrow aircraft and Iroquois engine known as the CF-105, the development of which has been continued pending a final decision. It has made a thorough examination in the light of all the information available concerning the probable nature of the threats to North America in future years, the alternative means of defence against such threats, and the estimated costs thereof. The conclusion arrived at is that the development of the Arrow aircraft and the Iroquois engine should be terminated now.

"Formal notice of termination is being given now to the contractors. All outstanding commitments will of course be settled equitably. Having regard to the information and advice we have received, however, there is no other feasible or justifiable course open to us. We must not abdicate our responsibility to assure that the huge sums which it is our duty to ask Parliament to provide for defence are being expended in the most effective way to achieve that purpose."

With those words, it was all over for the Avro Arrow program. Its cancellation eventually signalled the demise of A. V. Roe Canada, one of Canada's most important technology-based companies.

First flight of the Avro Arrow, piloted by Janusz Zurakowski. The aircraft on final approach to landing passed over the Malton home of the Avro Company.
March 25, 1958 / Hugh Mackechnie

On October 4, 1957, the same day as Sputnik 1 was revealed to the world, another important event was taking place in Malton, Ontario, at the Avro Canada Plant. After years of design and construction, the Avro CF-105 Arrow was officially rolled out in front of an estimated 12,000 proud employees and guests. Less than two years later, the Avro Arrow program would be dead and nearly all the employees fired.

1957 / National Archives

THE END OF A.V. ROE CANADA

A. V. Roe Company directors, led by Gordon, immediately fired nearly 14,000 employees. However, approximately 4,000 senior engineers and technicians were rehired within a few weeks for work on other projects handled by Avro Aircraft Limited and Orenda Engines Limited, including the Avrocar. Some of these workers were ultimately given the task of cutting up the six completed Arrows and the others on the production line, as on April 18, 1959, the government had ordered all aircraft (RL-201- 205 had already flown), plans and equipment destroyed. As Palmiro Campagna notes in *Storms of Controversy*, "The paper trail clearly shows that it was not Dief who ordered the scrapping of the aircraft. He did though follow the advice of two people, George Pearkes and Charles Foulkes, the Chairman, Chiefs of Staff. The documents show it was these two individuals who really orchestrated the cancellation."

David Mackechnie, in a 1999 correspondence, noted that "on the day the destruction began, Defence Minister Pearkes was asked by the press if it was true that the Arrows were being destroyed. He answered no. That very day, my father, Hugh Mackechnie, came home from work with photographs of the aircraft being destroyed! The next day Pearkes rose in the House of Commons to correct himself and say that yes, it was true, the Arrows were being cut into scrap. In truth, much more than that was happening. Crews were going all over the plant gathering plans, drawings, photographs, negatives and films—anything relating to the Arrow to be destroyed. There was to be no record left that the aircraft had ever existed.

"The destruction of all this material can be put this way. Looking back on this extraordinary event, the scrapping of the Arrow seems an act of either inspired malevolence or of criminal stupidity. A mocking epitaph to the work of the men and women who built her."

From 1949, when the Avro CF-105 Arrow was initially proposed, until the Canadian government's controversial cancellation of the project in 1959, the Avro Arrow program was one of great promise but unfulfilled objectives. It was undoubtedly one of the most advanced jet interceptors in the world, but owing to the prohibitive costs of development, it was an extremely costly military venture for Canada. With the changing political and military policy considerations that emerged in the late 1950s, the Avro Arrow was doomed. Many Canadians bemoaned the cancellation of this incredible aircraft, the devastation of Canada's largest aviation company and resulting exodus of Avro Canada scientists and engineers. Most of these staff members went to the United States to continue their work in the aerospace field, but it was a disaster for Canada's aviation industry, practically ensuring that future military aircraft would have to be purchased abroad.

Like most of the projects the Avro Canada company was undertaking in 1959, the Avrocar project and the people who worked on it were destined to be part of the fallout of the cancellation of the Avro Arrow project. No one felt that more keenly than its designer, John Frost.

CHAPTER THREE

MAN WITH A MISSION: JOHN FROST

JOHN CARVER MEADOWS FROST ("Jack" to close friends) was an enigma in the story of the Avro VTOL projects. Both friends and enemies recognized the genius and visionary aspects of the man, yet he had many detractors, including those he most respected—his fellow engineers.

When Frost had come to Canada, he had already been acknowledged as a gifted aircraft designer in England. His introduction to aviation had come early in 1930, when his school Latin teacher took him up in a vintage Bristol Fighter. John Frost was born in Walton-on-Thames, near London, in 1915, and showed an interest in the sciences at St. Edward's School, Oxford, where he graduated

with honours in mathematics, chemistry and physics. Frost also went to the top of his class in Latin, partially as an affirmation of his debt to his Latin teacher.

His aeronautical career began in the 1930s as an apprentice for Airspeed Limited, before he moved on to the Miles, Westland, Blackburn and Slingsby companies. In 1937, Frost had designed the fuselage of the new Westland Whirlwind fighter. At Blackburn, he had been involved with the design and construction of their prewar wind tunnel. While working for Slingsby Sailplanes from 1939 to 1942, he met his future wife, Joan, who had worked in the Slingsby Design Office as a technical artist. Frost also designed the Slingsby

Hengist, built in small numbers as one of the RAF's wartime troop-carrying gliders used in the Normandy landings. One of its ingenious innovations was the use of a rubber bag rather than a conventional undercarriage.

In 1942, Frost's work, however, began to be noticed when he joined the de Havilland Aircraft Company (United Kingdom), builders of the famed Mosquito bomber and fighter. In the war years, the de Havilland company was an exciting, innovative concern, and the ideal place for a young aviation engineer to mature. During his tenure, Frost began to put forward a number of unique ideas, including a tip-jet-driven rotor helicopter. He continued his research privately

J. C. M. FROST TIMELINE

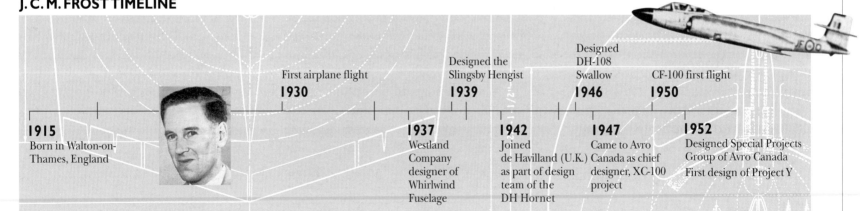

First airplane flight
1930

Designed the Slingsby Hengist
1939

Designed DH-108 Swallow
1946

CF-100 first flight
1950

1915
Born in Walton-on-Thames, England

1937
Westland Company designer of Whirlwind Fuselage

1942
Joined de Havilland (U.K.) as part of design team of the DH Hornet

1947
Came to Avro Canada as chief designer, XC-100 project

1952
Designed Special Projects Group of Avro Canada
First design of Project Y

and, with a group of friends, including fellow engineer T. Desmond Earl, built a scale model to test his helicopter theories.

Frost was responsible for a number of unique contributions to de Havilland designs. As one of the senior members of the design team, he designed a unique flap system for the Hornet fighter, the follow-up to the Mosquito. Later, as one of the team of designers on the DH-100 Vampire fighter, he was responsible for the design of its original flaps, dive brakes and ailerons.

DH-108 "SWALLOW"

Frost had then become heavily involved in one of the most important new developments of the time—swept wings and a tailless configuration on a jet fighter. Designer and company founder, Sir Geoffrey de Havilland, had already begun the DH-106 Comet development process and was considering that radical configuration for the world's first jet airliner. Frost was appointed project engineer on the DH-108, which was a derivative of the Vampire fighter. The Vampire had been one of the first Allied jet fighters in the Second World War, but other than its plywood construction, patterned on the Mosquito, the diminutive fighter was mainly conventional in design. With only a team of eight to ten draftsmen and engineers, Frost created a phenomenal aircraft, by marrying the front fuselage of the Vampire to a swept wing and short, stubby vertical tail to make the first British swept-wing

DH-108 "Swallow"
c. 1979 / via Aeroplane Monthly

jet, soon unofficially known as the "Swallow." The sleek and elegant experimental DH-108 was to serve as a test "mule" to investigate stability and control problems for the new Comet airliner.

On May 15, 1946, a mere eight months after Frost had a go-ahead on the project, the DH-108 first flew. Company test pilot and son of the builder, Geoffrey de Havilland Jr., flew the first of three prototypes and found the Swallow extremely fast — fast enough to try for a world speed record. A DH-108 did set a world's speed record at 973.65 kilometres per hour (605 m.p.h.) on April 12, 1948, and later became the first jet aircraft to exceed the speed of sound. The first DH-108, TG-283, was alleged to have suddenly jumped from Mach .98 to Mach 1.05 while being test flown by famed test pilot, John Derry, on September 9, 1948. Derry's passage

through the sound barrier, which he stated occurred during an uncontrolled dive, remains unofficial, since a recording camera was inoperative at the time. However, the seminal event in the DH-108's short life span had already occurred; while practising for an upcoming run at a new speed record, Geoffrey de Havilland Jr. died on September 27, 1946, when his DH-108 broke up in the air at or near the speed of sound.

Frost's work on supersonic projects was part of a worldwide race.

THE RACE FOR MACH ONE

The end of the Second World War had seen a great technological leap in aviation, as new propulsion systems based on rocket and jet power were introduced. With the successful operational use of the German Messerschmitt Me 163 rocket-powered interceptor and especially the twin-engined jet fighter, the Messerschmitt Me 262, conventional piston-powered aircraft were superceded. Both aircraft were amazingly fast and pushed the flight envelope into the reaches of the unknown.

Their designs also pointed the way forward on swept wings. As early as 1935, Prof. Adolf Büsemann of the German Luftfahrt-forchungsamt (Aeronautical Research Establishment) had suggested that wings "swept back" would reduce drag at the "sound barrier." This mysterious barrier had been the reason for many of the problems experienced by piston-engined fighter aircraft during high-speed dives in the Second World War. High-performance piston-engined fighters such as the Supermarine Spitfire and the North American P-51 Mustang had neared what was then known as "compressibility." This was the point at which the compression of the surrounding air would make the aircraft shake, and pilots found it nearly impossible to control the plane. In many instances, not only had controls "frozen," but the aircraft had fallen apart due to the violent buffeting at the speed of sound.

German research on swept wings influenced postwar fighter designs, but Great Britain emerged from the Second World War with a decided head start in jet technology. It was the only Allied power to have had a jet fighter operational in squadron strength before the war's end—the straight-winged Gloster Meteor.

The de Havilland Vampire was another British design that saw service in the immediate postwar era, and the Vampire had shown great potential for development. From that basic design came the swept-winged de Havilland Venom, DH-110 (a successor to the Vampire) and de Havilland (later Hawker-Siddeley) Sea Vixen, as well as the experimental DH-108. Tragically, after the loss of all the ill-fated de Havilland DH-108s and three test pilots and then the DH-110 prototype and pilot, John Derry, at the 1952 Farnborough Air Show (the aircraft disintegrated in flight, killing its pilot and twenty-eight spectators), no major British aviation manufacturer continued supersonic development in the 1950s.

Although Great Britain had pioneered many of the earlier efforts in supersonic flight, official interest in supersonic aircraft development had waned late in the 1940s. In February 1946, the British government cancelled the promising Miles M.52 project, based on a straight-winged bullet-shaped profile. All research data on this program, including the innovative "all-moving tailplane" for positive control at supersonic speeds, was turned over to the United States.

The sound barrier was officially broken on October 14, 1947. U.S. Air Force Capt. Charles E. Yeager, flying in a rocket-powered Bell XS-1 research plane over Muroc Dry Lake, California, became the first person to officially pass through the sound barrier when he achieved a speed of 1,100 kilometres per hour (700 m.p.h.), or Mach 1.06.

The National Advisory Committee for Aeronautics (NACA), the precursor to NASA, had shepherded the XS-1 project. The Bell rocket plane was not swept-winged, but like the Miles research plane, it was a streamlined "bullet," patterned after the shape of a .45-calibre bullet (known to go supersonic in flight). The aircraft, coincidentally, also featured an all-moving tailplane that allowed it to pass through the sound barrier safely.

However, increased structural integrity and swept-wing designs allowed even the marginally powered post-war jets to approach the speed of sound. Production jet fighters such as the North American F-86 Sabre pushed toward the sound barrier on swept-back wings. The Sabre and other contemporary fighters such as the Mikoyan-Guerich MiG-15 could achieve supersonic speeds in a dive. But in Canada, a more conservative approach had been employed in creating this country's first jet fighter.

John Frost from a news magazine.

c. 1959 / unknown

Opposite: John Frost with General A. G. Trudeau, U.S. Army.

c. 1956 / Avro Aircraft Ltd.

CANADA

In 1947, shortly after completion of the design of the Swallow, Avro Canada had persuaded John Frost to join their new design team as a designer of its first jet fighter. To him this was an ideal opportunity—a promising project to work on and a chance to get away from the depressing conditions of postwar Britain. At the time, his wife, Joan, was living in the North of England while Frost worked at Hatfield, near London. Accommodations for many young couples were similarly strained.

XC-100

On June 14, 1947, the Avro Canada design team met their new project designer. Frost and his wife had arrived at Malton at an extremely precarious point in the design of the XC-100. After eighteen months of development, the

new jet fighter had entered the mockup stage. Years later, Frost admitted that he was surprised by the crude wooden mockup that looked so different from his beautiful Swallow. He made a decision to alter the aircraft design, which immediately brought him into conflict with Chief Aerodynamicist Jim Chamberlin.

Basically cleaning up the fuselage, Frost set out to change the design subtly. Even though he wanted to use a swept-wing design, the aircraft, now called the CF-100, advanced to prototype stage in the same basic straight-winged, twin-engined configuration. Later in December 1950, Frost proposed a transonic follow-up to the CF-100—the swept-wing CF-103. It proceeded to mockup stage but was cancelled after Zurakowski dived the CF-100 Mk. 4 prototype to supersonic speeds. Although the CF-100 prototype was now a much sleeker shape, Frost still considered the design awkward, remarking in the 1979 *Daily News*, "It was a clumsy thing. All brute force."

While Frost was in England, conferring with members of the Hawker-Siddeley Group, Chamberlin made another alteration to the design, after wind-tunnel tests had shown that the centre of lift was too far forward. With approval from Chief Engineer Edgar Atkin, Chamberlin moved the engines back, but had to alter the wing spar to accommodate them. A nearly disastrous decision had been made, as the spar was now weakened and led to a flexible structure where there was heavy stress. In other words, the aircraft had a "soft" centre section in the wing spar.

PROBLEMS

With Atkin in Chamberlin's camp, Frost felt that his decisions were being challenged and that it might lead to potentially dangerous situations with the CF-100. With the wing-spar problem unsolved, the first flight of the CF-100 took place on January 19, 1950, with Bill Waterton, chief test pilot at Glosters (on loan to Avro Canada) at the controls.

Before Waterton returned to England, he flew with Frost in the second seat. To the test pilot, this was a revelation, and in *The Quick and the Dead*, he described Frost as "very much the keen English public schoolboy type," saying, "Here was another delightful contrast to England, where I was never able to find a designer with spare time enough to fly in his own creation." Frost was always a nervous flier, right from his first flight, but he considered it important to get a feel for the aircraft and its systems. He even tested the CF-100's ejection seat by becoming a test subject himself.

But the troubles with the CF-100 were still to weigh on Frost. The reason for his flight

Avro CF-100 Mk. 3T pre-production aircraft with dual controls and Orenda 2 engines being delivered to No. 3 AW (F) OTU in North Bay, Ontario, July 1952. c. July 1952 / via CAF

with the test pilot on the eighth flight, on March 13, 1950, was to see for himself the extent of the wing flexing.

Early flights revealed the great potential of the aircraft, but also showed that the flaw in the spar was dangerous. In September 1950, during a flight at the Canadian International Air Show at the Canadian National Exhibition (CNE), Waterton heard what he later described in his autobigraphy as a "violent crack: a sharp thunderclap of sound clearly audible above the engine and wind noise." Eventually the spar was corrected with a fix designed by Waclaw Czerwinski, the group leader in the stress office at A. V. Roe Canada.

Generally, Frost was considered a gentleman and a negotiator rather than a fierce competitor in the office-politics game. As fellow engineer, John Conway, observed, "John was a very modest man and I think very talented and certainly very cordial." But Frost now felt pressure from his superiors at Avro Canada. With the crash of the second CF-100 prototype and the release of production CF-100 Mk. 2s and 3s to the RCAF without final modifications to the spar, the CF-100 was not really ready for use—two years after its maiden flight.

REMOVAL

Reacting to criticism levelled at A. V. Roe Canada by the Canadian government and indirectly by the RCAF, Sir Roy Dobson made critical changes in the management and engineering teams in 1952. As Ken Caroline, one of the engineers from Avro (United Kingdom) observed, "It was not good for the firm to have all those conflicting personalities around and the management should have sorted them out, although I think they were probably more responsible for what happened in the end."

After reviewing reports from Stuart Dobie, a trusted Dobson man, and Fred Smye, the general manager, Aircraft Division, Dobson reassigned Atkin to the position of technical director or advisor (more of a lateral move, but nonetheless, he was removed from the day-to-day operations). Later in August 1952, Atkin left to take a position at Grumman Aviation in the United States.

In early 1952, Frost was also removed as the project designer of the CF-100, when Jim Floyd took over responsibility as chief engineer for the main aviation programs—the C-102 Jetliner, the CF-100 fighter and the new CF-105. For Frost, the decision was almost a reprieve, as he was allowed to set up a Special Projects Group to look at advanced aircraft designs. He had already begun work on a new project that would become his passion in the years to come.

FLYING SAUCERS

Les Wilkinson, in 1991, had described this period of change at Avro Canada. "Frost had given considerable thought to the many reports, both old and new, of unidentified flying objects in the sky (UFOs), more commonly called flying saucers...." And at the head office, A. R. (Ron) Williams recounted in 1976 that "the idea of building something that eventually got tagged a flying saucer grew out of a hobby of an Avro engineer named John Frost."

Frost was fascinated by reports of UFO sightings and made an effort to investigate ones that were reported. "What he was looking for was something that couldn't be explained by optical illusion, shadows on clouds, an over-active imagination, a con artist or whatever," said Williams.

"Frost had an instinctive feeling that perhaps someone somewhere had developed what came to be known as a flying saucer. Out of two hundred or more sightings he investigated, he found only two that could not be explained away by any of the above reasons. Both were in Europe—in the area of Germany. He concluded, rightly or wrongly, that there was a good chance the Germans with the advanced aeronautical technology they displayed during the war— rockets, buzz-bombs, et cetera—which was far ahead of the British and the Americans; that perhaps the Germans had built and were experimenting with a saucer-like vehicle."

THE UFO PHENOMENON

At the Pentagon, reports of UFOs had led to the first official U.S. study, launched on January 22, 1948. "Project Saucer" was the nickname given by the American public, but its real name, Project Sign, was kept secret.

The most famous incident that had introduced the term "flying saucers" had already taken place. When Kenneth Arnold reported his June 24, 1947, daylight sighting of nine circular-shaped objects near Mount Rainier, a newspaper reporter, Bill Bequette, covered the story for his paper in Oregon and sent it on to the Associated Press. Subsequent articles called the objects flying saucers. Arnold had only described their movements as similar to that of a saucer skipping across the surface of water, but the more engaging term seemed to fit better with the public. The era of flying saucers had begun. Arnold's story later appeared in *Fate Magazine.*

The first case that Project Sign investigated involved a fatality. United States Air Force (USAF) Capt. Thomas Mantell was leading a flight of three F-51 Mustang fighters on a routine flight over Godman Field in Kentucky on January 7, 1948, when a "silver teardrop" was witnessed by many people on the ground. During the pursuit, Mantell had crashed, apparently due to a lack of oxygen.

Project Sign had no idea at the time what this UFO was, but offered the suggestion that the pilot had been chasing the planet Venus, which often was the cause of reports. This explanation backfired, and led to what Project Saucer described as "simmering public discontent, leading to the birth of the belief that there is a government cover-up to hide the truth from the general public."

It is now known from declassified files that the UFO that Mantell had chased was a secret naval project using a Skyhook balloon. Unfortunately, the launch was considered so secret that not even the members of Project Sign were aware of its existence.

Another troubling case followed, known as the Chiles-Whitted incident of July 24, 1948. An Eastern Airlines passenger DC-3 was in near collision with a rocket-like object as it flew across the skies above Montgomery, Alabama. In a 1956 Report on Unidentified Flying Objects, Edward Ruppelt, a former head of the UFO investigation Project Blue Book, said that the sighting had a profound influence on Project Sign personnel. This one incident can be argued to be the single most important sighting in the U.S. Air Force's records, according to the influence it had on Air Force thinking.

A top-secret "estimate of situation" report was sent on August 8 by concerned Project Sign officials to Gen. Hoyt S. Vandenberg, head of the United States Air Force. This report argued that UFOs were real and extraterrestrial, but it was immediately rejected by Vandenberg, who sent it back saying that he required physical proof. However, with increased Cold War tensions and the Korean War, concerns about UFOs continued, and USAF Director of Intelligence Maj. Gen. Charles P. Cabell ordered a new UFO project in 1952.

From 1947 to 1969, the air force investigated unidentified flying objects under the auspices of Project Blue Book.

The task of identifying and explaining UFOs continued to fall on the Air Material Command at Wright-Patterson Air Force Base. With a small staff, the Air Technical Intelligence Center (ATIC) tried to persuade the public that UFOs were neither extraterrestrial nor unusual events. For the next thirty years, Projects Sign, Grudge, and Blue Book, headquartered at Wright-Patterson, Ohio, set the tone for the official United States

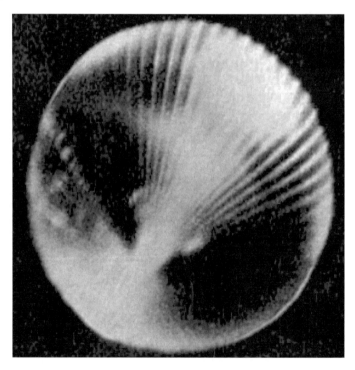

U.S. Navy Project "Skyhook" balloon.

c. 1947 / MUFON

government position regarding UFOs. Air Force Secretary Robert C. Seamans Jr. terminated Project Blue Book on December 17, 1969, when the air force claimed it could no longer justify the project for national security reasons or scientific study. Of a total of 12,618 sightings reported to Project Blue Book, 701 remained unidentified. After closing Project Blue Book, the USAF has not publicly acknowledged any further interest in UFO sightings.

AVRO'S FIRST STEPS

Far less has been published about the origins of the Avro's secret flying-saucer projects. Recently, while doing research at Canada's National Archives, historian Larry Koerner says he "came across a file containing a document which provided an account of a meeting that may shed some further light on the development of the Avrocar. The meeting, which took place in the then West Germany during 1953, at a Canadian government installation, was attended by a German aviation engineer along with officers of the RCAF, RAF, British Intelligence Services and John Frost, an Avro Canada executive. The purpose of the meeting was to give Mr. Frost, who was already working on the design of a ground-cushion vehicle, the opportunity to cross-examine the German engineer.

"This man claimed to have been working on a similar type of aircraft for the German government between 1944 and 1945 at a site near Prague, in what is now the Czech Republic. Moreover, the German asserted that not only had such a saucer-like vehicle been built, but it had also been flight tested. However, he also said that, at the end of the war, both plans and the aircraft itself had been destroyed. Unfortunately the file in question provided no further indication as to how useful this information was to either Avro Canada or to the British and Canadian governments."

Earlier than this, Frost had begun to investigate some of the ideas he had hypothesized would lead to a dramatic breakthrough in aviation design. The first-known step towards this occurred one day in late 1951, when Frost walked up to Bob Johnson, one of the shop superintendents involved with CF-100 production, and gave him a sketch. Frost required a small metal disc of about 9 centimetres (3.5 in.) in diameter by 5 centimetres (2 in.) thick, with a series of small scoops all around, and a shaft with ball bearings at its centre (something like a small disc wheel). He also asked for an air pressure gauge and the control valve needed to control the pressure and volume of air passing over the disc.

Wilkinson, in a 1991 interview with Johnson, noted that "the shop superintendent queried John as to where this fitted on the CF-100 and was told, never mind, just book its manufacture to something on the CF-100." At this point, even though the workers went ahead and manufactured the part, more than one of them was puzzled by the interest shown by Frost in what they considered a toy or plaything. Johnson was openly wondering if the stress of the CF-100 problems was getting to Frost. "John Frost was seen later with his clipboard, taking notes while spinning the disc at varying speeds by the use of an air hose pointed at different angles at the small scoops on its circumference. With the disc shaft clamped in a vice, he used a tachometer to record the disc rpm." Des Earl, now one of the aerodynamicists at Avro, says he was intrigued by the way Frost was able to "turn this thing around with the gyroscope running and it would float around the room in a most fascinating way."

"It was soon after this, that Frost presented his ideas to Avro management at Malton," reported Wilkinson. Frost proposed that Avro start an experimental project on its own.

Ron Williams reported in the *Winnipeg Tribune* in December 1976 that "it was not a case of Frost indulging in a personal whim. The idea of a saucer-like flying machine had revolutionary implications then and still does. A conventional aircraft is very inefficient, aerodynamically, and like a bumble bee, there's no way it should fly. It only does so because of the wing, which gives it lift, and the engine's power to overcome the drag of the fuselage, the load, the tailplane, the stabilizers, fins and the engines."

And other aviation designers were also exploring unusual designs.

CHAPTER FOUR

STRANGE SHAPES IN THE SKY

WHILE THE USAF had officially studied reports of unbelievably high-performance flying saucers in the late 1940s, as early as October 1947 the USAF Air Materiel Command issued a document called the "Air Intelligence Guide for Alleged 'Flying Saucer' Type Aircraft," or "Flying Saucer EEI" (for essential elements of information). EEI was a term used in Air Technical Intelligence to describe the technical details of a foreign aircraft that Wright Field desired from U.S. sources overseas. The Air Materiel Command drafted a formal "Collection Memorandum," describing in detail these characteristics, and send it to air attachés in overseas embassies. The Flying Saucer EEI became Collection Memorandum 7, and went to all of the significant United States embassies worldwide, including Canada.

Engineers around the world had already shown interest in the aerodynamic and structural properties of such a shape. As early as 1935, Henri Coanda in France had designed a Lenticular Aerodyne that closely resembled the shape of a flying saucer. It used the "Coanda effect" to create vertical lift without forward motion, as well as to control the aircraft. In the United States, a lengthy and detailed patent (U.S. No. 3,103,324) applied for by the Lockheed Aircraft Corporation in 1953, described, as reported in *Air Progress* in 1964, an "aircraft of circular plan-form and of bi-convex vertical cross section." Along with vertical takeoff and landing capability, the aircraft used a combination of gas-turbine and ramjets to fly at Mach 4 speeds at 30,500-metre (100,000 ft.) altitude.

The patent lists several properties that suit a saucer to these goals. The shape, it claims, provides excellent structural rigidity, aerodynamic stability in vertical ascent and descent, and room inside for large amounts of payload and fuel. Furthermore, its smooth profile and unbroken leading and trailing edges were thought to lend it inherent aerodynamic efficiency. "There is no record of Lockheed's radical craft ever getting off the

UNCONVENTIONAL AIRCRAFT TIMELINE

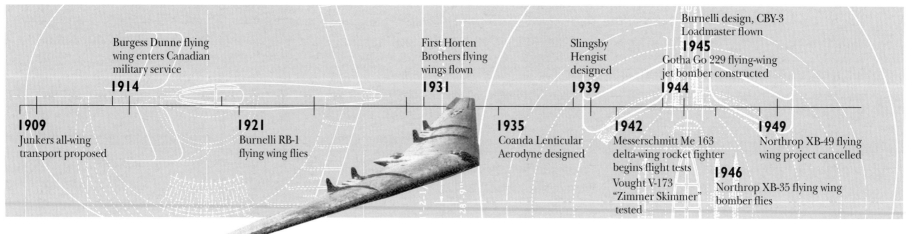

Burgess Dunne flying wing enters Canadian military service
1914

First Horten Brothers flying wings flown
1931

Slingsby Hengist designed
1939

Burnelli design, CBY-3 Loadmaster flown
1945
Gotha Go 229 flying-wing jet bomber constructed
1944

1909
Junkers all-wing transport proposed

1921
Burnelli RB-1 flying wing flies

1935
Coanda Lenticular Aerodyne designed

1942
Messerschmitt Me 163 delta-wing rocket fighter begins flight tests
Vought V-173 "Zimmer Skimmer" tested

1946
Northrop XB-35 flying wing bomber flies

1949
Northrop XB-49 flying wing project cancelled

drawing board," reported Abe Dane in *Popular Mechanics* in 1995. But besides the saucer designs, other intriguing shapes were also being investigated.

FLYING WINGS

Since the early days of aviation, aircraft designers have dreamed of creating the ideal design, marrying the load carrying of the fuselage with the lift of the wings—a "flying wing." The flying-wing concept dates back to 1909, when Prof. Hugo Junkers of Germany envisioned a large flying-wing airliner capable of carrying hundreds of passengers. Other designers, such as England's John Dunne, produced designs incorporating the flying wing, including the Burgess Dunne of 1914, which became Canada's first military aircraft in service. Then a flying-wing renaissance of sorts began in the inter-war years, as British designs such as the Westland Aircraft Pterodactyl and the General Aircraft series of glider prototypes were tested and flown.

BURNELLI'S FLYING WINGS

In the United States, Vincent J. Burnelli (1895–1964) theorized that the fuselage could supply more than 50 percent of an airplane's lift if it were airfoil shaped. With the additional lift, the plane could operate with smaller engines and a lighter fuel load than aircraft of more conventional design. Burnelli's first flying wing, RB-1, created in 1921, was a twin-engine, fabric-covered

Burnelli Flying Wing Cancargo CBY-3 Loadmaster on a test flight in 1947.

1947 / Smithsonian Institute

biplane that incorporated many of the unique characteristics that would be associated with Burnelli-designed transports—including a large airfoil-shaped fuselage that featured twin power-plants side by side at the edge of the fuselage. Later versions would utilize metal construction and incorporate further aerodynamic and structural improvements.

For the next five decades, Burnelli's ideas were reflected in a continuing series of transport prototypes that were seen as ground-breaking examples of technology. The advantages of the Burnelli design not only included performance, such as greater lifting and load-carrying capability, but also reputedly the safety advantages of a stronger fuselage section and the placement of the engines farther from the passenger compartment in the event of a fire or crash.

The CBY-3 Loadmaster, an evolution of the earlier UB-14, built in 1945 by the Canadian Car and Foundry Company in Montreal, was the last of the Burnelli designs. It was powered by a pair of 1,200-horsepower Pratt and Whitney R-1830 Twin-Wasp engines. With a length of just over 17.37 metres (57 ft.), a wingspan of 26.2 metres (85.9 ft.) and a gross weight of 12,247 kilograms (27,000 lbs.), the twin-tailed transport could carry twenty-four passengers or operate as a rugged bush plane. Although Burnelli's aircraft were often on the world stage—setting records and garnering publicity—he was never able to find the backing for a production run.

Burnelli, however, was not the only designer to explore unusual shapes.

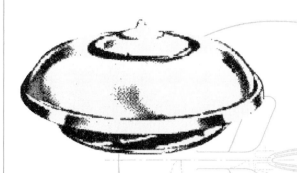

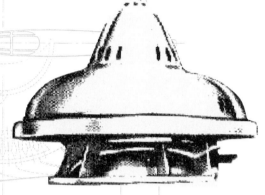

German "Krautmeteors" based on the work of scientists Bellonzo, Schriever, Miethe and Victor Schauberger. Schauberger developed the "flying hat" type disc; the final version was the Bellonzo-Schriever-Miethe Diskus.

c. 1945 / *Der Spiegel* article dated March 30, 1950

THE GERMAN CONNECTION

German aeronautical technology is the source of many myths about the origin of flying saucers. Beginning in 1944, United States Army Air Forces (USAAF) Intelligence Service created special groups of language and technical-research specialists to recover the technological hardware and research data relating to advanced German weapons. The Allies sent teams to Europe to gain access to enemy aircraft, technical and scientific reports, research facilities, and weapons, to learn about Germany's technical developments.

In the United States, the Air Technical Intelligence (ATI) Teams were trained at the Technical Intelligence School at Wright Field, Ohio. The ATI teams competed with thirty-two Allied technical-intelligence groups as well as the Soviets to gain information and equipment recovered from crash sites. As the war concluded, the various intelligence teams, including the ATI, shifted from tactical intelligence to post-hostilities exploitation investigations. On April 22, 1945, the USAAF

combined technical and post-hostilities intelligence objectives under the Exploitation Division with the code name Operation Lusty (code for Operation of gathering LUftwaffe Secret TechnologY).

Capturing V-2 rockets, the most obvious and well-known example of German scientific expertise, was the beginning. Through an intelligence estimate known as the Oslo Letter, passed to the Allies via a Norwegian source, the Allies were made aware of other weapons under development and in operation by Axis powers. These included jet engines, cruise missiles, radio-controlled bombs, huge guns, intercontinental ballistic missiles, rocket launchers, new radar systems, long-range bombers and torpedoes, as well as research

in many other areas of weapons development. The German advanced technology included vertical-takeoff aircraft; among the most secret items reportedly captured were plans for flying discs that were at first called "Krautmeteors." Apparently, these aircraft were built as early as around 1933 and were in production in 1940. The scientists involved in these projects were Giuseppe Bellonzo, Dr. Walter Miethe, Rudolph Schriever, and Victor Schauberger.

The competing Allied and Soviet effort was dedicated to getting hold of much more than data and equipment: German scientists were also prey. Operations Overcast and Paperclip were examples of Allied efforts to obtain German experts. The scientists involved were on the "black list" of wanted technical specialists drawn up by Allied intelligence operatives and hunted down by a combination of FIAT and CAF teams from June 1944 on. Featured on the list were the Horten Brothers, Dr. Focke and Prof. Alexander Lippisch.

HORTEN BROTHERS FLYING WINGS

Although the Burnelli designs proved the concept of a lifting-body fuselage, they were not a true flying wing, as they often had separate tail surfaces on twin booms. In Germany, in the 1930s and 1940s, the Horten Brothers, Walter and Reimar, built a succession of true flying-wing designs that were quite advanced and on the cutting edge for their day. Beginning with the Ho I sailplane in 1931 and continuing through with the Ho IX in 1944, the series of elegant flying-wing designs was destined to be a tantalizing glimpse into the future. The 1945 Ho VIII design was a 48.15-metre (158 ft.) wing span, six-engine transport, which was reborn in the 1950s when Reimar Horten built a version of this aircraft for Argentina's Institute Aerotecnico. It flew on December 9, 1960, but the project was shelved thereafter due to technical problems.

The 1944 Ho IX (also known as the Gotha Go 229) was flown in January 1945. It was the first Horten design intended for combat, but it arrived too late to see service. Due to wartime shortages, the jet-powered (by two Junkers Ju 004 Bs) Ho IX was designed with a metal frame and plywood exterior. When the Allies overran the factory, the almost-completed Ho IX V3 (third in the series) was shipped back to the United States. Today, it resides in the National Air and Space Museum in Washington, D.C.

After the war, Northrop Aircraft Company in the United States acquired the Horten Ho VI "Flying Parabola" glider for analysis. However, the link between these two had come about earlier, in 1941, as the Horten brothers were helped in their bid for German government support when Northrop patents for their N-1M flying wing were publicized.

FOCKE-WULF VTOL PROJECTS

From the mid-1930s, there was significant interest in Germany in both vertical-takeoff-and-landing and circular-wing aircraft. Prof.

Heinrich Focke was particularly interested in emerging helicopter and autogyro technologies and was involved in the design and production of the FW 6, Fa 223, Fa 226, Fa 283 and Fa 284 models during the war. The creation of the jet engine also encouraged him to design a turbo-shaft propulsion system.

The Focke-Wulf Triebflugel design was an imaginative VTOL point-defence fighter. It used a three-blade rotor wing with adjustable rotor pitch, with the rotors mounted at the centre of gravity of the aircraft. Three 840-horsepower Lorin ramjet engines mounted at the rotor tips powered the aircraft. These ramjets did not operate at speeds below

Focke-Wulf FW "Triebflugel." 2000 / Mario Marino

Right: Artist's conception of the Gotha Go 229 in operational service. 1999 / Dragon (DML)

300 kilometres per hour (186 m.p.h.), so the rotor had to be driven by a fuselage-mounted booster engine at low speeds and at takeoff and landing. The Triebflugel was to take off and land in a vertical position, resting on a large central tail wheel. The design proceeded to scale models that were successfully flown.

In 1939, Focke also patented a flying wing of a saucer-type design with enclosed twin rotors. The exhaust nozzle forked in two at the end of the engine and ended in two auxiliary combustion chambers located on the trailing edge of the wing. When fuel was added to these combustion chambers they would act as afterburners to provide horizontal propulsion to the design. The control at low speed was achieved by alternately varying the power from each auxiliary combustion chamber. Both of these unusual wartime designs were examples of Germany's technological achievements, but the end of the war brought Focke's work to a halt.

ALEXANDER LIPPISCH'S TRIANGLE PLANES

One other flying-wing-type plane was used by the German Luftwaffe—the 1942 Messerschmitt Me 163 rocket-powered interceptor and its intended successor, the Messerschmitt P.1111, a turbojet-powered fighter. The design was based on the work of one of the leading aviation experts in Germany—Alexander Lippisch. Lippisch, whose work at the Gottingen Aviation Institute was legendary, had started his development of all-wing gliders in 1926. His revolutionary DM series of small, triangular aircraft was built and flown in conjunction with students at Darmstadt and Munich Universities.

Lippisch's impact upon postwar aviation

Sack AS6 "saucer" craft partly designed by Dr. Alexander Lippisch. This aircraft was built in 1940 and tested in April 1944 by Luftwaffe Squadron JG 400 at Brandis, Germany. The sole prototype of the AS6 was destroyed when the Luftwaffe retreated from Brandis. c. 1944 / Air International

cannot be underestimated, and at war's end he was engaged in supersonic research. Plans and models of his P-12 supersonic fighter were shipped back to the U.S. for analysis. But his most advanced design was undoubtedly the Lippisch Supersonic Flying Wing, which, although never built, strongly hinted at the triangular aircraft of the 1980s and 1990s. In later years, when Lippisch

moved to the United States, his work involved research in ground-effect vehicles, which were evaluated by Avro Canada.

SACK AS6

Another German project partly designed by Dr. Alexander Lippisch was the troubled Sack AS6. It was an all-wing circular aircraft built in 1940 by Arthur Sack, a Bavarian farmer and aircraft modeller. After some model-flight testing, the Messerschmitt company built a prototype, using the canopy and landing gear from a Bf 109. The fuselage was incorporated in a circular wooden wing, earning it the nickname "Fliegende Bierdeckel," or "Flying Beer Tray." From April 1944, JG 400, the same squadron flying the Lippisch-designed Messerschmitt Me-163 evaluated the Sack AS6 at their base in Brandis, Germany. The AS6 performance did not meet expectations, but before improvements could be made, the Luftwaffe lost all interest in the project. The sole prototype of the AS6 was destroyed when the Luftwaffe retreated from Brandis in 1945.

THE AMERICAN CONNECTION

During the same period, in the United States, a number of revolutionary projects exploring all-wing designs had been built. In the mid-1930s, the Arup S1, S2, S3 and S4—looking very much like what became the "Zimmer Skimmer," but with a single centre-line "puller" propeller—were flown as flying billboards and test aircraft.

THE "FLYING PANCAKE"

Before the Second World War, Charles Zimmerman, a research engineer for NACA, had come up with a disc-shaped design that promised to be fast and to have short takeoff and landing ability. His "Zimmer Skimmer" was designed as a high-speed interceptor for the United States Navy. The design was characterized by an oblong disc shape, with a canopy on top near the front, twin rudders and two small ailerons in the rear, and twin booms extending forward from the left and right sides of the disc with huge counter-rotating propellers on each. The fuselage was the wing, but was much thinner and wider than later lifting-body experiments. The Skimmer sat at a 22-degree angle on a spindly looking arrangement of tricycle undercarriage. High speeds, in the order of 800 kilometres per hour (500 m.p.h.), and the ability to vertically take off and even hover, were some of the claims made for this design.

Chance-Vought built the V-173 technology demonstrator, which made its first flight on November 23, 1942. The flight lasted only thirteen minutes but was entirely successful, and testing continued. One of the later test pilots was Charles Lindbergh, who was an enthusiastic supporter. In July 1944,

the navy ordered two prototype Chance-Vought XF5U-1s, nicknamed "Flying Pancakes," each equipped with a significantly more powerful engine — a 1,600-horsepower Pratt and Whitney R-2000-2(D). The two new planes were manufactured from metalite, a composite material made by sandwiching layers of aluminum and balsa wood. The first XF5U-1 was ready for flight in August 1945, but was delayed by a lengthy redesign of the propellers and gearing system. They were

actually overpowered, and required a clutched gearing system to vary propeller speed in flight. In addition, a geared propeller/synchronizer was also installed.

By 1948, an XF5U-1 was finally ready to fly, but technology had passed the plane by, as jet fighters were already flying at over

Chance-Vought V-173 technology demonstrator — the "Zimmer Skimmer" on a test flight.

c. 1942 / Air Enthusiast, 1973

950 kilometres per hour (590 m.p.h.). The Chance-Vought XF5U-1 underwent taxi tests and even "hopped" into the air, but both examples were broken up at the end of the program. The V-173 survived and was put into storage at the naval station in Norfolk, Virginia. Today, with its vertical fins and "flying tail" removed, it is in storage at the Smithsonian Institute's National Air and Space Museum warehouse (the Paul E. Garber Facility) in Silver Hill, Maryland.

THE NORTHROP FLYING WINGS

The most influential American all-wing designs came from the Northrop Company. Jack Northrop, one of America's most inventive and imaginative designers, had been experimenting with flying-wing designs since the early 1920s. Northrop proposed a design, the XB-35, in response to a wartime United States Army Air Force requirement for extremely long-ranged, heavy bomb-load aircraft that could fly from North America

to Germany and back, carrying 4,500 kilograms (9,920 lbs) of bombs. The Northrop design had four engines, each driving two

The YB-49 Flying Wing over the Mojave Desert, 1947. A flying wing configuration, as used in the Northrop YB-49, eliminates drag-producing junctions. It represents a major departure from the classical aircraft design because now the wing/fuselage provides lift, volume, and stability.

1947 / Northrop Aviation

counter-rotating pusher propellers along the same shaft.

Northrop's first development of the concept came with the N-1M, nicknamed "the Jeep," which was tested in the Roseman Dry Lake in the Mohave Desert from July 1940 to early 1942. The small, 1,814-kilogram (4,000 lb.) experimental craft, with a wingspan of 11 metres (36 ft.), had two pusher propellers and space for one pilot. Its first public flight made the newsreels. The wings were altered significantly as testing went on; for instance, the drooping wingtips were discarded early on. The N-1M still exists, and has been restored. It is now sitting in a Smithsonian storage hangar, painted in its original brilliant yellow.

The follow-up Northrop N-9M was a one-third-scale, wood-structured test bed/trainer with two engines. It first flew successfully on December 27, 1942. Three other N-9Ms were built, with the N-9M test program completed in October 1944. Another parallel Northrop Second World War flying-wing project included the turbojet-powered XP-79 "Flying Ram," a rocket-powered interceptor that was designed to literally slice off the tail of enemy aircraft with its heavily reinforced wing. Other Northrop designs included the rocket-powered MX-324, which first flew on July 5, 1944, and the XP-56, a pusher-engined flying-wing fighter. This unique design, which also made several test flights in 1943 and 1944, featured two counter-rotating propellers along the same shaft.

Northrop was contracted by the United States Army Air Force Materiel Division to build one XB-35 with a 52.4-metre (172 ft.) wingspan. On June 25, 1946, the XB-35 was at last ready to fly at Hawthorne Field, California—the Northrop company field. The USAAF provided Northrop with a small-scale production order to continue the flying-wing development. But attempts to simplify the operation of the troublesome and unreliable propeller system were generally unsuccessful, so Northrop decided to replace the piston engine/propeller arrangement with eight jet engines, and continued work on the plane, now renamed the YB-49.

The second YB-49 produced was the first to fly, on October 21, 1947, flown by Maj. Robert Cardinas, the USAAF test pilot assigned to the Northrop program. On April 26, 1948, the YB-49 flew 6,437 kilometres (4,000 mi.) with a 4,535-kilogram (10,000 lb.) payload, on a circuitous route that took it as far east as Phoenix and as far north as San Francisco. In June 1948, a YB-49 flown by USAAF Capt. Glen Edwards crashed on a routine test flight, and although the specific cause of the crash was never determined, structural failure was the most likely reason. The impact of the crash was soon to be felt in Northrop.

As development proceeded, the military expressed an interest in the YRB-49, a reconnaissance version (with two extra jets), and placed an order for thirty. In January 1949, this order was cancelled. In February 1949, the remaining YB-49 flew from Muroc Air Force Base to Andrews Air Force Base in the record time of just over four hours. The famous YB-49 "over the Capitol" photos are from this flight. President Harry S. Truman toured the plane's interior on the ground, and then the aircraft headed back to California. During the flight, six of the eight engines failed due to oil failure, and the YB-49 had to make an emergency landing in Winslow, Arizona.

Later in 1949, the last flying YB-49 was damaged during high-speed taxi tests when the undercarriage collapsed. In November 1949, the United States Air Force cancelled the last part of the YB-49 contract, that of converting the remaining partially completed XB-35s to jet power. The last eleven XB-35 hulls in varying states of assembly were rolled out onto the flight ramp outside of the factory, lined up, photographed and broken up for scrap in a scene resembling that of the later Avro Arrow program's demise.

Jack Northrop resigned from the company he had built after the YB-49 was cancelled, and left the aircraft industry entirely. In the mid-1970s, NASA sent him a letter stating that they were reexamining the flying-wing idea as a "stealth" program. In April 1980, Northrop received some form of vindication for his earlier work with flying wings when he was shown a model of the future B-2. The Northrop B-2 Spirit today has exactly the same wingspan as the YB-49 and is considered the modern rebirth of the flying wing.

At Avro Canada, John Frost continued a similar effort in exploring radical new ideas.

CHAPTER FIVE

PROJECT Y: A NEW DIMENSION

THE SPECIAL PROJECTS GROUP

FROM 1951 ON, John Frost had devoted his energies to revolutionary approaches in aeronautical design as the head of a special research group in Avro Canada. Years later, fellow Avro Canada engineer Bill Procter described the first days of the formation of the group, saying, "Every so often a project comes along that is a quantum leap ahead of what people are working on at the time." Frost had such a project in mind.

In early 1952, Frost hand-picked a team of eight engineers and draftsmen that included engineers T. D. "Des" Earl, Waclaw Czerwinski, Al Wheelband and Alex C. Bryans, to create the original Special Projects Group. He tended to bring together people like himself, the dreamers and the rebels. Ray Takeuchi, a later member, described the Special Projects Group, noting that "John Frost really got a good team together and was one of the boys—not a head-table type."

As chief designer, Frost was considered one of the "boffins," but his method of operation was vastly different from other engineers. As Desmond Earl commented in an obituary on Frost in *Canadian Aeronautics and Space* in 1980, "John Frost had an intense belief in the power of thought, and would take endless trouble reiterating a design idea looking for flaws. Since he always did this privately before discussing it he was hardly ever caught out advocating the impractical."

The team was first housed in a building across the street from the Avro plant, in the penthouse executive dining room. "Guards on the door, locked doors, special passes... we were not exactly ostracized but we played our own little tune in the corner of a very large company," commented Al Wheelband in 1983. The Special Projects Group operated as a distinct entity of its own—able to move in any direction. Their secretive work resembled that of the famous "Skunk Works" of Lockheed Aviation (later Lockheed-Marietta), which turned out "black projects" such as the U-2, SR-71 and F-117 stealth fighter.

PROJECT Y TIMELINE

February: Research begins on pancake engine 1952	**July: Design of spade-shaped Project Y** 1952	**December: Frost presents ideas at Avro (United Kingdom)** 1952	**February: Project Y media reports** 1953	**May: Project Y evaluation made at Royal Aeronautical Establishment, Farnborough** 1953	**September: Project Omega investigated** 1953	

1952 Special Projects Group formed	**1952** April: First ideas on circular disc shape, company financing provided	**1952** November: Favourable analysis in Mordell report	**1953** Ground-cushion effect discovered January: Project Y put on hold	**1953** April: Project Y mockup shown to Field Marshall Montgomery	**1953** June: Project Y jet-flap wind tunnel tested by Avro (United Kingdom)

INITIAL DESIGN

One of the keys to the design Frost had in mind was a radically different engine. In an internal A. V. Roe Canada document, "Description and Thoughts on the Turbo Disc," dated February 7, 1952, he briefly described a simple form of gas-turbine engine that would form a halfway step between the ram-jet engine and the centrifugal engine as originally conceived by Whittle (inventor of the jet engine).

Its principle aim was as follows:
1. A thrust-to-weight ratio of at least nine to one.
2. The development of high thrust and comparative efficiency with no forward speed.
3. The attachment of moderate to high compression ratios with low centrifugal stresses.
4. The elimination of turbine discs and blades.
5. The use of simple materials and manufacturing processes.

The engine had the appearance of a hollow disc, 61 centimetres (24 in.) in diameter and 5 centimetres (2 in.) thick, rotating on a central bearing arrangement. Air would be drawn into the disc through a central air intake, burnt internally and expelled around the circumference from six equally pitched tangential nozzles.

The disc would be made up of two main parts:
1. An inner disc rotating clockwise with the central eye intake as an integral part and twelve straight radial vanes sandwiched

between the two walls of the disc.
2. An outer disc positioned about the inner disc but rotating counterclockwise on a common centre with the inner disc carrying on its circumference the six equally spaced nozzles, pointing tangentially rearwards relative to the direction of rotation.

Frost sent this report, along with preliminary drawings, to Prof. Donald L. Mordell, professor of engineering at McGill University in Montreal, in February 1952, and Mordell

First test model of the hovering disc concept that John Frost used in the first experiments.

c. 1952 / Avro Aircraft Ltd.

began an intensive review of the project. During his assessment, Mordell conferred with Gerald Bull of the Canadian Armament and Research Development Establishment (CARDE), a man who later gained fame as the inventor of the "Supergun."

In April 1952, Frost co-authored a paper with T. D. Earl entitled, "Proposal for a Gas

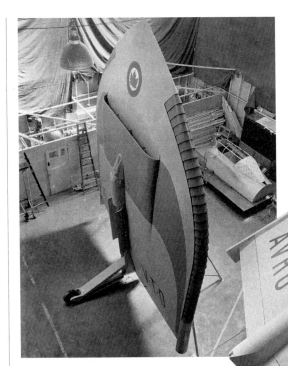

Left: Project Y mockup was in a heavily guarded part of the Avro plant.   c. 1953 / via Des Earl

Below: Project Y mockup was based on the earliest "Avro Ace" design.   c. 1953 / via Des Earl

Turbine Propelled Aircraft of Circular Plan Form." In it, his design idea was described further: "It is now possible to illustrate further development; show constructional detail of a proposed design and support estimated performance with calculated weight based on stress analysis. The layout permits very high power to be built into a very small aeroplane in a very simple manner. Although new production techniques will need to be evolved, the elimination of many of the features indispensable to a more conventional aeroplane makes for economical manufacture and maintenance. This aeroplane will have about 850 lb. S.L. [sea level] static thrust per sq. ft. of aircraft frontal area (a typical 6,000 lb. bare axial engine without cowling produces only 625 lb./sq. ft.): and it will have about 1.5 lb. S.L. static thrust per lb. gross take-off weight; therefore its performance must surpass that of any known type of aeroplane.

"Fundamentally, the design is unorthodox in two respects:

a) It is proposed to control the aeroplane by altering the direction of thrust forces.

b) It is proposed to stabilize the aeroplane by means of a powerful gyroscope—the large diameter engine rotor."

However, in a period of three months, the project changed from circular to spade or "D" shape, based on the work of Czerwinski, and became known as Project Y. Frost authored another report for Avro Canada in July of that year, entitled, "Project Y: An All-Wing Supersonic Aeroplane." Copies of the reports were circulated to Avro (United Kingdom) and sent to the United States joint chief of staff. With this new project, the Special Projects Group was energized. As Al Wheelband commented, "Frost and the whole team were extremely enthusiastic...we all realized, including John Frost, that there were many problems involved. John Frost was a man who didn't bother about the long-sighted problems; he only bothered about the one that was today and we'd worry about tomorrow's problems tomorrow. He tackled this job by biting a little piece off every day and solving a problem every day and worrying about tomorrow, tomorrow."

By April 1952, A. V. Roe Canada financed Project Y as a company project, but with the intention of eventually producing an operational fighter for the RCAF. The design was nicknamed the "Praying Mantis," "Flying Manta," "Manta Ray" or "Stingray," because of its unusual shape and stance. In some official documents, the original design of Project Y was also designated Avro Ace (and also identified as Project Y1 or Y-1). The new design was actually a spade-shaped flying wing. It was small, with a span and length of about 12 metres (39 ft.). At the sharply cut-off tail was a large, elliptical exhaust nozzle with deflectors for control, which routed the flow from a central turbo compressor. A large pancake turbine engine was to revolve around a vertical axis inside the wing. The disc-shaped rotor of the engine had blades mounted on either side of the rotor. The inboard section of the rotor was supported by conventional bearings, but the outboard section was to use air bearings for support as well as for cooling. The rotor also would act as a giant gyroscope to provide inherent stability to the aircraft. Exhaust gases were to be discharged from numerous exhaust ducts for propulsion.

Although the Avro Ace incorporated a dual-cockpit arrangement and two long undercarriage legs on top and bottom of the fuselage, the later and final shape of Project Y featured a single-pilot cockpit with a teardrop-shaped canopy at the top centre of the aircraft. The pilot had 360-degree visibility to the horizon but was blind under the edges of the aircraft. A clear panel under the cockpit floor allowed the pilot to monitor takeoffs, landings and ground handling. With its single landing gear extended, Project Y sat at an approximately 45-degree angle on its tail. Most engineers thought that a vertical launch might have been possible and explored a near vertical (70-degree angle or more) stance at first, but a rolling takeoff was judged more feasible. Frost reasoned that taking off and landing in this position would be difficult, if not out-and-out dangerous, and later the entire concept of a tail-sitter aircraft was reconsidered and abandoned.

A great deal of preliminary work was taking place at this time. On August 21, 1952, British Patent 892,401 was issued for the design. And although the contents were already known, on September 29 and November 1, 1952, the Mordell report was officially presented in two parts to Avro Canada. Mordell's assessment was that "the present design appears to be aerodynamically satisfactory...performance at high flight speeds is good."

In December 1952, Frost and two other engineers from Avro Canada, Earl and John Dubbury, visited A. V. Roe (United Kingdom) to discuss Project Y and were invited to conduct wind-tunnel tests at Woodford. This was to confirm the design of four aircraft variants: (1) basic aircraft (A/C), (2) development A/C, (3) development A/C with reheat (afterburning) and (4) military version. While in England, they visited Farnborough to present their Project Y concept, where their reports were evaluated by Avro engineers and compared to research already initiated by the company. The Avro 724 was already on the drawing boards and represented a similar concept, although Frost's engine design and propulsion/stability system was vastly different. The Avro design was a tailless delta tail-sitter that was designed as either a single jet engine or two-engine interceptor. A model of the jet flap that would be instrumental in propulsion and control of Project Y was later wind-tunnel tested in the Avro Woodford tunnel in Manchester, England, in early 1953.

The specifications for Project Y were established:

Dimensions

length	7.8 metres (25.6 ft.)
span	6.4 metres (21 ft.)
height	1.55 metres (5.08 ft.)
gross area	116 metres^2 (380 ft.^{2})

Crew	1 pilot
Armament	two Blue Jay missiles carried externally
Engine Power	186,425 kilowatts (250,000 hp.)

Performance Data (Estimated)

maximum speed	2,400 kilometres per hour (1,500 m.p.h.)
ceiling	30,500 metres (100,000 ft.)
range	1,255 kilometres (780 mi.)
rate of climb	30,500 metres per minute (100,000 ft.)

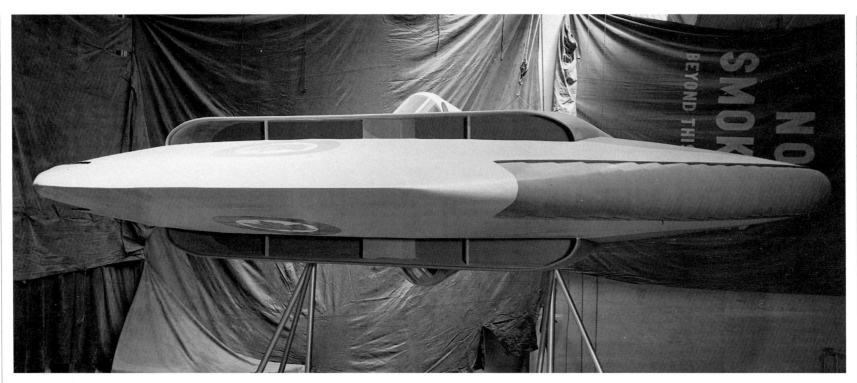

The Canadian government funding, supplied by Dr. Omond M. Solandt and Dr. J. J. Green of the Canadian Defence Research Board, had provided $379,000 for research and development of Project Y and later developments. But in January 1953, Project Y was put on hold, awaiting further funding. Avro had estimated that at least a three-year development cost of over $200 million (Canadian) would be required. The early work was carried out in total secrecy; Alex Raeburn, Avro's workshop superintendent at the time, was quoted in a 1999 article by Julian Borger in the *Guardian* as having said, "It was so secret that when Frost would come to the welding shop, he would sketch the piece he wanted on some paper and, when we had finished, we had to put the sketch in a special garbage bag."

COANDA EFFECT

During this period, while investigating various circular models with peripheral jets to check the Coanda theory, Frost stumbled across the ground-cushion effect. He would later remark, in a 1961 article in the *Canadian Aeronautical Journal*, "It is unfortunate that our sights were set on developing a supersonic vertical-takeoff aircraft when Avro stumbled on the ground cushion, otherwise we might have paid more attention to its possible uses as an

Project Y mockup under construction. The view is "edge-on" and shows the dual cockpit arrangement that was part of the earlier Avro Ace design.

c. 1953 / via Des Earl

amphibious surface vehicle...we missed its potential as a method of improving the performance of water-borne craft."

The most known, studied, and applied discovery of Henri Coanda is the Coanda effect—the tendency of a fluid to follow a curved surface. Coanda stated that the first time he realized something about what would become known as the Coanda effect was while he was testing his reactive airplane,

Coanda-1910. After his plane took off, Coanda observed that the flames and burned gases that went out of the engine tended to remain very close to the fuselage. Studies lasting more than twenty years were carried out by Coanda and other scientists, and the phenomenon was recognized as a new one, and identified as the Coanda effect. On October 8, 1934, Coanda applied for a patent for a procedure and device for the deviation of a fluid inside another fluid. The Coanda effect has had many important aeronautical applications, including changing the thrust direction for modern aircraft (thrust reversal), lowering the noise level for reactive engines (or for experimental stands) and increasing the lift of lifting surfaces.

Based on the Coanda effect, in 1935 Coanda designed his Aerodina Lenticulara, a flying machine that resembles a flying saucer. Coanda himself considered that this could be the most important application of his effect for aviation of the future. Harry Stine reported in a 1967 article in *Flying*, that at a symposium organized by the Romanian Academy, Coanda said, "These airplanes we have today are no more than a perfection of a toy made of paper children use to play with. My opinion is we should search for a completely different flying machine, based on other flying principles. I consider the

Project Y mockup showing a part of the wing section that was left open to show the interior structure.

c. 1953 / via Des Earl

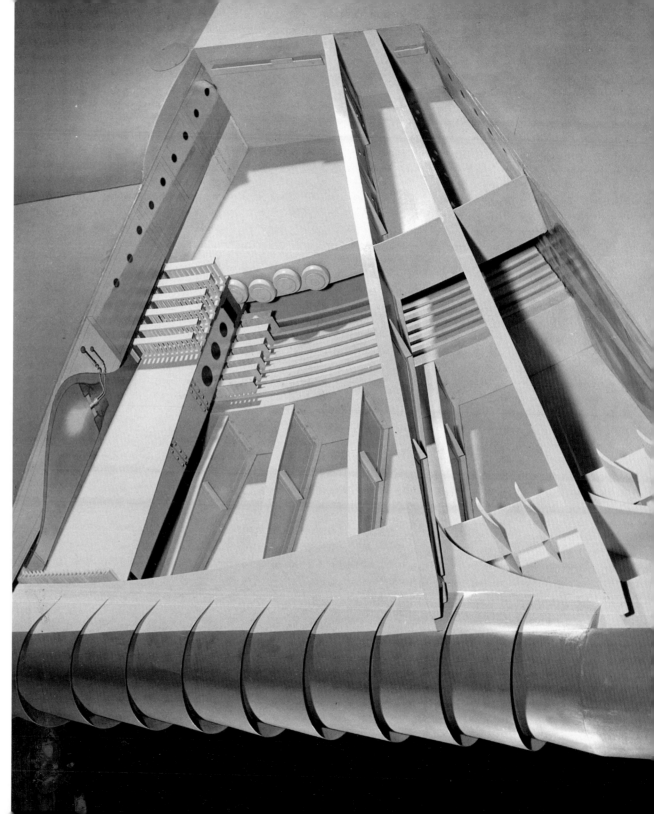

Project Y "jet flap" model that was sent to Avro (U.K.) for wind tunnel tests.

c. 1953 / via Des Earl

aircraft of the future, that which will take off vertically, fly as usual and land vertically."

Project Y was exactly that type of new flying machine. Williams noted in the *Winnipeg Tribune* in December 1976 that "to try and convince some of the doubting Thomases, the theory was tested with 18-inch models. Power was simulated with compressed air carried to the model through small diameter rubber hoses. The jet thrust was expelled around the periphery. It was amusing to see Frost or someone else, using remote controls flying the model saucers around his experimental lab. The thought occurred to me often afterwards when the project was dead, that we missed the boat. We should have gone into the business of making toy flying saucers!

What a hit they would have been with kids and adults." As Frost developed further studies, his ideas on revolutionary vertical-takeoff systems led to the patent of the "air cushion effect" (United States Patent 376,320, August 23, 1953). The patent is often described as the "Frost patent."

By February 1953, the Special Projects Group had moved to a new location, in the old Orenda Building across from the main plant, one that was more conducive to design and testing, and away from watchful eyes.

THE BURST OF PUBLICITY

The existence of the secret project was eventually leaked to the press. The *Toronto Star* carried a feature article on February 11, 1953, under the headline "Takes Off Straight Up, Report Malton 'Flying Saucer' to do 1,500 MPH." The article reported that "highly secret reports of a Canadian 'flying saucer' are circulating—among British and U.S. defence scientists.... Western scientists must consider the possibility that Soviet Russia has carried similar developments to a more advanced stage.... Crawford Gordon Jr.—No Comment." On February 12, 1953, the *New York Times* reported, "Govt. studying fighter able to takeoff vertically and fly at speeds topping 1000 mph; disc type craft based on gyroscopic principle with jet powerplant revolving round stable control central cockpit." The *Toronto Star* disclosed on February 16, 1953, that C. D. Howe, minister of defence production, informed the Canadian House of Commons that "the government was constantly studying new concepts and new designs for fighters...adding weight to reports that Avro is even now working on a mockup model of a flying saucer."

On February 27, 1953, the A. V. Roe Canada president noted in the company's house organ, *Jet Age*, that "like all aircraft companies who want to stay in business, we are directing a substantial part of our efforts towards new ideas and advanced designs. One of our projects can be said to be quite revolutionary in concept and appearance. The prototype being built is so revolutionary that when it flies all other types of supersonic aircraft will become obsolescent. That is all that Avro Canada are going to say about this project."

In early 1953, a wooden mockup of Project Y was constructed behind high walls and under very tight security in the flight-test hangar at Avro Canada. The mockup, painted with RCAF markings, was being readied for a highly public visit to come shortly. On April 21, 1953, the *Toronto Star* again raised the question of the project when it stated that Britain's "Field Marshal Montgomery... became one of a handful of people ever to see Avro's mockup of a flying saucer reputed to be capable of flying 1500 miles per hour. A guide who accompanied Montgomery quoted as describing it as fantastic.... Security precautions surrounding this super-secret are so tight that two of Montgomery's escorts from Scotland Yard were barred from the forbidden screened-off area of the Avro plant."

Air Vice Marshal D. M. Smith stated that what Field Marshal Montgomery had seen was the preliminary study of construction plans for a gyroscopic fighter that could take off vertically and fly at a speed of 2,400 kilometres per hour (1,500 m.p.h.). A gas turbine would revolve around the pilot, who would be positioned at the centre of the disc. But as Al Wheelband remembered, Avro insiders knew that the carefully leaked information was part of the political intrigue to get more money for the project.

On April 24, 1953, the *Toronto Star* confirmed its February story, stating that many of Canada's best aeronautical engineers were working on a flying disc made of metal, wood and plastics, intended to be the weapon of the future. Rumours about the project had circulated for months at the Malton plant without official confirmation. Evidently, the mockup was still doing its job in stirring up interest in the project. It was to remain at Avro Canada until 1954, when it was scrapped, long after the original Project Y concept had changed to a flat-riser type.

THE OMEGA

Later, on September 17, 1953, the *New York Times* followed up its initial articles with a report that "U.S. Scientists and Canadian Officials confer on secret disc-shaped jet fighter able to reach 1500 mph after vertical takeoff." Finally on October 2, 1953, the *New York Times* stated, "A. V. Roe seeks backers for prototype of disc-shaped jet fighter."

Also in 1953, the *Royal Air Force Flying Review* featured an article, "Man-made Flying Saucers," publishing schematics of what the American press called the "Omega." The design was reportedly to test a new formula for construction of supersonic interceptors. It was small, with a span and length of about eleven metres (36 feet). About twenty air-intake slots were provided along the leading edge to supply the buried turbine. At the sharply cut off tail was a large, elliptical exhaust nozzle with exit deflectors for yaw

control, which routed the flow from a central turbo compressor. Exhaust gases were to be discharged from numerous exhaust ducts for propulsion.

A teardrop-shaped, single-pilot cockpit was located in the top centre of the aircraft, with 360-degree visibility to the horizon but blind under the edges of the aircraft. Although no details were provided, the large turbine engine was shown to revolve around a vertical axis inside the wing. The question of the exact type of propulsion remained, but in the January 5, 1954, issue of *Aeroplane*, in an article titled "Avro Canada's Omega," it was suggested that the design was a radical centripetal turbine-exhausting gas that expanded in a collector. The *London Times* also carried short articles on the Canadian saucer program on April 22 and 23, 1953.

Although the Omega project garnered headlines, it never went beyond the design stage; essentially it was an interim design that was based on Project Y and had not involved the vertical-rising or VTOL approach, now a distinguishing feature of all the later Project Y2 derivatives.

CHAPTER SIX

VERTICAL TAKEOFF AND LANDING

PROJECT Y2

By the end of 1953, Avro Canada Project Y had evolved into a different aircraft, now known as Project Y2. Based on research by John Frost on the ground-effect characteristics of a vertically rising and landing vehicle, Project Y2 also benefitted from wind-tunnel tests that showed the circular-shaped disc planform was more efficient for structural simplicity and was lightweight. The new design not only had the capability of supersonic speed but also the advantages of a true VTOL aircraft.

VTOL

VTOL stands for vertical takeoff and landing, which is a type of vehicle that uses the thrust of air to lift itself straight up. A helicopter is a rotary-wing type, compared to a VTOL aircraft, which, as noted in *Air and Space* in 1999, "eschewed the complications and performance limitations of rotor blades, which must hinge, twist, and flex to simultaneously act as lifting and thrusting surfaces in forward flight." For such aircraft to be developed, two requirements are necessary. The first is a powerplant that can develop a thrust greater than the aircraft's weight, and the second is a means of controlling the stability of an aircraft in vertical flight, when thrust and weight are in unstable opposition. Since a VTOL can lift its own weight, it can be built in any shape. Examples of VTOLs today are the Hawker-Siddeley Harrier "Jump Jet" fighter and the Bell-Boeing V-22 Osprey.

According to a *Look* magazine article in June 1955, one problem identified by Brig. Gen. Benjamin Kelsey, deputy director of research and development of the USAF, was

VERTICAL TAKEOFF AND LANDING TIMELINE

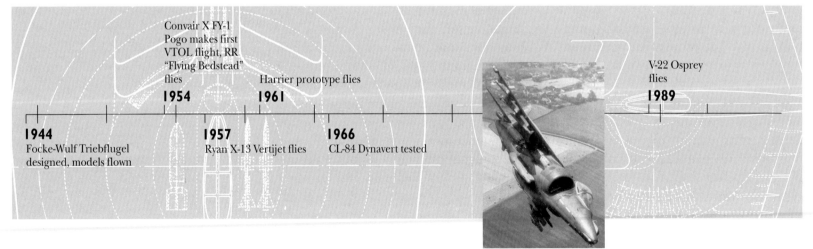

Convair X FY-1 Pogo makes first VTOL flight, RR "Flying Bedstead" flies
1954

Harrier prototype flies
1961

V-22 Osprey flies
1989

1944
Focke-Wulf Triebflugel designed, models flown

1957
Ryan X-13 Vertijet flies

1966
CL-84 Dynavert tested

AMES RESEARCH CENTER

Left: XV-3 VTOL airplane/helicopter hovering at NASA Ames Research Center. 1961 / Lee Jones

Below: V-22 Osprey testing. U.S. Navy, Marine Corps and Air Force Osprey is a tiltrotor aircraft with an 11.6-metre (38 ft.) rotor system and engine/transmission nacelle mounted on each wing tip. When taking off and landing vertically, the V-22A can operate as a helicopter. Once airborne, the nacelles rotate forward 90 degrees for horizontal flight, converting the Osprey into a high-speed, fuel-efficient turboprop airplane. 1999 / Boeing Public Affairs Department

that "airplanes today spend too much time gathering speed on the ground and not enough flying in the air." He pointed out that today's fighters need extremely long runways, and there are few in existence that are now long enough. These few, and the concentration of the planes using them, provide a worthwhile target for an A-bomb. With a single blow, the enemy might cripple a substantial portion of air defence.

Kelsey's view was that "planes that could take off vertically would not need long runways, which cost millions of dollars. They could be dispersed widely and safely.... What

U.S. Air Force began testing the Ryan X-13 Vertijet at Edwards AFB in 1955. By 1957, when Ryan test pilot Pete Girard made this first flight, the Vertijet featuring a vertical takeoff and landing and a transition to horizontal flight.

April 11, 1957 / Ryan Aviation

are the requirements of an ideal defense fighter? 1) Ability to take off and land vertically; 2) high speed of over Mach 2 (more than 1500 mph); 3) high rate of climb; 4) excellent manoeuvrability; 5) heavy armament; 6) ability to operate at 60,000 feet (18, 288 m)."

TAIL-SITTERS

The advent of the turbojet engine, with its superior power, spawned a handful of projects centred on creating a VTOL fighter that could operate without a conventional runway or even an aircraft carrier deck. The first series of projects were reminiscent of the wartime Focke-Wulf Triebflugel design and the original Project Y-1. They were known as "tail-sitters." The Convair XFY-1, the Lockheed XFV-1 and Ryan X-13 were the most successful examples of the design concept, and in the mid-1950s they briefly achieved prominence.

Earlier in 1951, the U.S. Navy became interested in a turbine-powered VTOL fighter that could operate from the decks of small ships. Its sole virtue was that it didn't need a runway or even a large carrier deck surface. These airplanes, designed to perch on their tails, were never meant to be air-superiority fighters but point-defence interceptors. Their contra-rotating paddle blades went to work purely as huge mixmasters, powering the aircraft to speeds as high as 900 kilometres per hour (560 m.p.h.). As noted in *Air and Space* magazine in 1999, "The tail-sitters transitioned from helicopter to airplane by simply pushing over from the vertical ascent to conventional horizontal flight."

The Lockheed and Convair prototypes were both based on the 5,500-shaft-horsepower (4,100 kw) Allison XT40. Lockheed's tail-sitter, the XFV-1 "Salmon," ended up making six untethered flights, for a total of two hours and twenty-one minutes. It flew a lot more, but accomplished somewhat less than the Convair XFY-1 "Pogo," which made the first VTOL flight in history on November 2, 1954. By the end of its testing programs, the Convair design had reached an enviable record of reliability and had met most of its performance objectives, but ultimately the unstable flight characteristics of both fighters, especially in transition flying, made them impractical. Lockheed's designer, Kelly Johnson, simply called the XFV dangerous.

The advent of the turbojet engine, with its superior power, spawned a handful of projects centred on creating a VTOL fighter. The Ryan X-13 "Vertijet," which was powered by a non-afterburning 4,500-kilogram-thrust (10,000 lb.) Rolls-Royce Avon, was the first pure jet-powered VTOL aircraft. It needed only a trailer fitted with a gantry from which to operate. The United States Air Force began testing the aircraft at Edwards Air Force Base in 1955. On April 11, 1957, when Ryan test pilot Pete Girard made the first flight featuring a vertical takeoff and landing and a transition to horizontal flight, the aircraft had already made many successful conventional takeoffs and landings using a temporary landing gear.

The Vertijet detached from its launching ramp/truck, rolled 180 degrees and then pitched over into conventional flight. After its mission, it returned to its launch ramp for landing. The Ryan X-13 demonstrated controllability during low-level vertical-flight mode, however much of its success depended on the skill of the pilot, particularly in manoeuvring in the complex tail-first landing mode. As the aircraft balanced on the exhaust thrust of the Avon engine, a small thruster-control system allowed the pilot to maintain aircraft movement and direction. The X-13 was, in many ways, the most successful of the tail-sitter designs, yet the project was ultimately cancelled. Later designs such as the SNECMA C 450-01 met a similar fate.

FLAT-RISERS
Rolls-Royce Flying Bedstead

Jet engines still were the answer to VTOL needs. In England, by 1954, at Hucknall Air Force Base, a chapter in military aviation was to be written with the development of the thrust-measuring rig, a rather mundane and unglamorous technical name for what was to become better known as the "Flying Bedstead," the first step on the road to the Harrier. The Flying Bedstead was little more then a pair of powerful jet engines mounted in a large framework with their jet outlets directed downwards to give vertical thrust. Initial flights in 1953 were tethered or chained to the ground to limit the height of flight. The pilot of this test bed would control the stability of the machine by varying the flow through stabilizing nozzles mounted on outriggers. As Mike Rogers wrote in *Military Research Aircraft*, in 1989, one pilot described this technique as "trying to balance on top of four wobbly bamboo poles." The technique became easier as the control system was developed in the Flying Bedstead.

By 1954 the system had been developed sufficiently for the machine to achieve free flight on August 3, demonstrating that an aircraft could be designed that would take off and land vertically. Others, notably Hawker-Siddeley, developed the concept into airframes, and the famous Harrier was born, powered by a Rolls-Royce Pegasus engine, which was also development tested at Hucknall. Today, the VTOL combat-aircraft concept has its vindication in the Harrier.

Harrier

After much opposition in Great Britain and abroad, this aircraft proved itself in the

Rolls-Royce "Flying Bedstead" test-flying. The development of the Rolls-Royce Thrust Measuring Rig, a rather mundane and unglamorous technical name for what was to become better known as the "Flying Bedstead," the first step on the road to the VTOL Harrier. 1954 / Rolls-Royce Hucknall

Falklands War of 1982 and later in American operations in the Gulf War in 1991 and recent Balkan conflicts. Simply stated, Great Britain could not even have mounted the operation to retake the Falklands Islands had it not been for the existence of the Harrier. Without this aircraft, there would have been no air power available to British forces in the campaign, and the naval fleet available would have been at the total mercy of the land-based aircraft of the Argentine Air Force and Navy. In the Falklands, the Harriers of the Royal Navy and Royal Air Force achieved a twenty-eight to zero score in air combat against the Argentinean Mirage aircraft, believed at the time to be among the best aircraft in the world.

In the case of the United States Marine's AV-8 Harrier, it performed as a strike fighter and still maintained capability as a dog fighter in recent engagements. Additionally, what makes the Harrier a war winner is its capacity for doing VIFF (vectoring in forward flight)—the technique of rapidly changing the direction of thrust of the engine from horizontal to vertical during combat. The VIFF manoeuvre throws the aircraft out of the path of both attacking cannon fire and missiles. In no other way can a subsonic aircraft expect to be able to defeat one capable of twice the speed of sound.

Harrier GR7.

Convertiplanes

The attempt to combine helicopter and conventional aircraft in a transition-type aircraft led to the "convertiplane." In the 1950s and 1960s, manufacturers in the United States, Great Britain, the Soviet Union and Canada pursued the goal of a successful convertiplane. Some of the aircraft designs, such as the British Fairey Rotodyne, were more like helicopters with fixed engines. The Rotodyne briefly set world records in the 1950s but ultimately met the fate of many promising concepts when government support was withdrawn and the aircraft was scrapped. American manufacturers Bell, Curtiss-Wright, Hiller, McDonnell and Vertol also produced unusual convertiplane prototypes. The most successful American design was the LTV-Hiller-Ryan XC-142A, which had five flying examples that completed a thorough testing and evaluation program by the USAF but still were not put into production. A later effort, the Bell XV-15, however, was not only successfully evaluated but has resulted in the Bell-Boeing V-22A Osprey tilt-rotor aircraft now entering service in the United States Navy, Marine Corps and Air Force.

CL-84 Dynavert

In the 1960s, Canadair designed the CL-84 Dynavert to be an aircraft that could operate as V/STOL. It was able to hover like a helicopter (VTOL), or fly like a conventional aircraft with short takeoff and landing (STOL) capability. The tilt-wing CL-84 remains the most advanced of the convertiplanes. While the entire wing rotated through 90 degrees, to transition from vertical to conventional forward flight, its most innovative engineering was reflected in the flight-control system. This system allowed the pilot to use the stick and rudder pedals in the conventional manner to manoeuvre the aircraft—flying horizontally with the wings locked down—or vertically with the wings rotated up, or in transitional flight mode. A unique control-mixing box linked the ailerons, elevators, rudder and angle of the propeller blades, coordinating their movements and relationship to each other (control sharing), depending on the position of the wing.

Construction of the original prototype began in 1963 and was completed a year later. Hovering flight was tested in 1965, and flight in transitional mode was tested in 1966, before the prototype was lost in a flying accident. The Canadian government ordered three updated CL-84s, designated the CL-84-1, for military evaluation in 1968. They were fitted with mini gun pods near the fuselage. From 1972 to 1974, this version was demonstrated and evaluated in the United States aboard the aircraft carriers USS *Guam* and USS *Guadalcanal*, and at various other centres. These trials involved military pilots from the United States, the United Kingdom and Canada. Unfortunately, the first CL-84-1 was lost in a training accident during the trials when a propeller gearbox failed. But the pilots ejected safely.

Despite the aircraft being at the leading edge of technological innovation, there was little interest in the expensive development of V/STOL technology, particularly when helicopters could fulfill the VTOL role. The CL-84 never went into quantity production, and the program died for lack of military customers. A CL-84 is on display at the National Aviation Museum of Canada, in Ottawa. It was the second of the three CL-84-1s produced, and made 196 flights, totaling 169 flying hours. It was donated to the museum by Canadair in 1984. Other CL-84s exist at the Western Canada Aviation Museum and the Toronto Aerospace Museum. Ominously, the fate of the Dynavert was already mirrored by that of the Avrocar.

Canadair CL-84 Dynavert 8401 seen during hovering tests. It was the first of four CL-84 research/test aircraft.

1965 / Western Canada Aviation Museum

CHAPTER SEVEN

SELLING THE CONCEPT

THE AMERICAN INVOLVEMENT

The *New York Times* reported that a team of twenty-five U.S. defence experts visited the Avro Canada plant at Malton on September 16, 1953. Officially, the team was there to view the new CF-100 Mark 4 Canuck jet fighter and the naval radar installations at Ferranti Canada in Toronto. The team was headed by Lt. Gen. Donald L. Putt, head of the research and development command of the USAF. Members of the U.S. deputation included Maj. Gen. John McCormack; Dr. A. G. Hill, chief of the Lincoln Laboratory; and J. Marchetti, technical director of the Cambridge Research Center. The Americans conferred with Dr. O. M. Solandt, chairman of Canada's Defence Research Board; C. L. Drury, deputy defence minister; and Gen. A. G. McNaughton, head of the Canadian section of the United States-Canada Joint Defence Board. They were briefed on Avro Canada's Project Y2, a flat-rising, disc-shaped fighter design capable of supersonic speed.

Project Y2 was developed into two versions: Version 1 was based on the original pancake-engine concept, but was soon superceded by Version 2, a multi-engine aircraft, which would avoid concurrent development of the airframe and engine. Early in the design, considerations of safety were also addressed, as Project Y2 would be vulnerable to damage in the rotor area, causing a catastrophic loss of the aircraft and aircrew. A multi-engine configuration was considered the best means to maintain power and control if the aircraft were damaged in combat. Version 2 utilized eight Armstrong-Siddeley ASM Viper 5 jet engines in its initial proposal.

Avro had funded the initial Project Y2 development, assisted by money and support from Dr. Solandt of the Canadian Defence Research Board. But now, Solandt, through Gen. D. L. Putt, was instrumental in interesting the United States Air Force in Frost's work. A. V. Roe showed Putt and his party a series of proposals. Frost reportedly advanced the proposition that he had gone as far as possible with paper studies. The project had, however,

AVRO CANADA VTOL TIMELINE

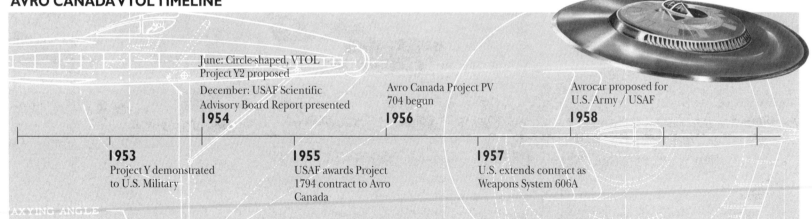

June: Circle-shaped, VTOL Project Y2 proposed

December: USAF Scientific Advisory Board Report presented
1954

Avro Canada Project PV 704 begun
1956

Avrocar proposed for U.S. Army / USAF
1958

1953
Project Y demonstrated to U.S. Military

1955
USAF awards Project 1794 contract to Avro Canada

1957
U.S. extends contract as Weapons System 606A

piqued the interest of the American military, and by July 1954, Project Y2 was known as "Project Ladybird" in the USAF. The NACA Lewis Propulsion Laboratory examined the Avro proposals and reported favourably in August. This report had a profound influence on the USAF decision to follow. In late August 1954, USAF Gen. O. P. Weyland, commander at Tactical Air Command, Langley Air Force Base, visited Avro and was given a thorough briefing on Project Y2. Before he left, he expressed his desire to join the venture.

As a final step, Putt requested a report on the merits of the Avro saucer project via Brig. Gen. (ret.) J. H. "Jimmy" Doolittle, the acting chairman of the U.S. Scientific Advisory Board (SAB). A select committee composed of Dean Soderburg, chairman of the Propulsion Panel and senior member of the SAB, Prof. John R. Markham of the Aircraft Panel and Mr. Allan F. Donovan of the Aircraft and Propulsion Panel reviewed the project. The committee focused on the nature of the new propulsion system. The report cautioned that "the invention involves a whole array of formidable problems of research and development...We recommend against any contractual support for this project until much greater potentialities have been demonstrated." With two conflicting opinions from the SAB and NACA to consider, Putt came down on the side of NACA.

In the House of Commons, C. D. Howe, the minister of trade, announced on December 2, 1954, that Canadian scientists had worked for about eighteen months on a flying-saucer project, but it was finally shelved. Howe said that the Avro Canada firm had planned the craft, but had dropped it. This statement may have been made to stop speculation about the aircraft or to disguise the true outcome of the project, although he declared, "We did the engineering on it and proved to ourselves that it would fly.... It would cost about one hundred million dollars to develop and did not seem sufficiently promising to be worth going with." Eventually, after spending about $2 million between 1952 and 1953, the Canadian government halted all funding, as the design effort was purchased outright by the USAF. Despite the pessimistic review by the SAB, and although a formal proposal was not given by Avro to the U.S. until the end of the year, the USAF took over funding for the Project Y2 design program and redesignated it as USAF Project MX-1794 in late 1954.

Why did the USAF become involved in Project Y2? It was obvious that the lure of the dramatic technological breakthrough was there, even though their own SAB report had emphasized that claims made by Avro

Lt. Gen. Donald L. Putt, head of the Research and Development Command of the U.S. Air Force, was a visitor to Avro and is photographed in the first Avrocar. He was the driving force behind the American military support of Avro's VTOL projects. c. 1958 / via Les Wilkinson

were unrealistic. In 1955, USAF Technical Report Number TR-AC-47 stated that "an examination of the AVRO proposal shows that the potential for a very high performance weapon system exists in the not-too-distant future.... This proposal offers a possible solution to the USAF requirement for achieving dispersed base operations."

PROJECT 1794

Further discussions were held with Lt. Gen. Putt through the DRB, and the result was the award of a $784,492.29 contract, AF33 (600)-30161, from the USAF on May 6, 1955. The contract was to extend through to August 1956 under the new project title Project MX-1794, later referred to as Project 1794. The contract provided for subsonic and hover tests in the Massie Memorial Wind Tunnel at the Wright Air Development Center (WADC) at Wright Patterson Air Force Base, Dayton, Ohio. Further supersonic testing at the U.S. Navy Research Wind Tunnel of the Massachusetts Institute of Technology (MIT) in Cambridge, Massachusetts, and various other tests back at Avro were also incorporated. As a means of meeting a United States Navy VTOL Visual Fighter Program (U.S. Navy Specification TS-140), Avro briefly resurrected Project Y and submitted a proposal on October 1, 1956, that was subsequently

Artist's conception of Project 1794 vehicles on a mission. Notice one on the ground in the background of the drawing. 1956 / Avro Aircraft Ltd.

rejected. Throughout the project, the U.S. Navy sent their representatives to project meetings and continued to maintain an interest in the Project 1794 supersonic studies through their involvement at MIT.

PROVING THE CONCEPT

Now unclassified, Technical Report Number TR-ΛC-47 was a joint ATIC-WADC report on Project Silver Bug, Project Number 9961. Released on February 15, 1955, and published by the Air Technical Intelligence Center at the Wright-Patterson Air Force Base, it revealed that the "Project Y2 design proposal incorporates a number of advance improvements brought about by the utilization of several radical ideas in fundamental areas which, as for the construction of a very large radial-flow gas turbine engine which, when covered, will form a flying wing with a circular planform, similar in appearance to a very large discus." USAF sources at the Pentagon stated that "all information regarding their relationship were classified and could not be divulged." But under pressure from the press, the Air Force issued a statement, as published in the *Montreal Star* on August 24, 1955, reading, "The Air Force has a research and development contract with the Avro Company of Canada to explore a new aircraft design concept."

This airframe and engine would have a circular planform; the outer perimeter of the aircraft was the exhaust nozzle of the engine and the thrust forces would be used

Project 1794 press release photograph.

c. 1956 / via Worldwide Photo B7120

for control of the aircraft. Air intakes were placed in the inner circle on the upper surface of the aircraft, for vertical takeoff, while additional air intakes were installed in the upper and lower forward-facing surfaces for forward flight. The aircraft was designed to fly edge-on to the wind instead of axially, as is the present practice in conventional aircraft design. The cockpit was located at the centre of the aircraft, with the airframe, fuel cells, and turborotor encircling the cockpit. This flat-riser aircraft allowed the elimination of landing gear, as it was designed for vertical takeoff and landing while in the horizontal-flight attitude. The flat-riser flight-takeoff technique was brought about by the peripheral exhaust, which produced a powerful ground-cushion effect.

Frost had three different wind-tunnel models constructed. A 1/6-scale, 1.524-metre (5 ft.) subsonic model with both intake flow and simulated jet thrust was tested in half-plane and full-plane forms at the 6-metre (20 ft.) WADC wind tunnel. A total of approximately 900 hours of subsonic wind-tunnel

testing was eventually completed from November 1955 to December 1961. The two supersonic wind-tunnel models (in both half-plane and full-plane versions), along with a separate model of the intake, were tested at MIT for over 250 hours. The models incorporated peripheral jets supplied by compressed air to blow upwards or downwards or be deflected rearward to simulate hover and flight. Results of the testing indicated that the subsonic characteristics were marginal due to the low-aspect ratio of the circular airfoil but that in supersonic flight, high aerodynamic lift/drag values in the order of five were achieved at speeds from Mach 1.5 to Mach 3. The wind-tunnel program provided a background in the aerodynamic properties of a circular planform that supplemented the only previous study by Zimmerman in the 1940s.

A research vehicle was proposed for the purpose of investigating stability, control and low-speed performance before development of a multi-engine operational aircraft. This prototype design would also investigate certain fundamental areas concerning aircraft behaviour, such as the ground-cushion effect. The next step was to build an actual aircraft.

Left and opposite page: Project 1794 1/6 scale half-plane wind-tunnel test model used for subsonic testing at MIT laboratory.

1956 / Avro Aircraft Ltd

Project 1794 specifications:

Dimensions

diameter	10.75 metres (35.3 ft.)
height	2.34 metres (7.7 ft.)

Weight

basic	6,200 kilograms (13,750 lbs.)
gross	9,000 kilograms (20,000 lbs.)
maximum	12,393 kilograms (27,322 lbs.)

Crew	1 pilot
Engine Power	six Armstrong-Siddeley Viper 8 engines at 1,900 kilograms (4,188 lbs.)

Performance Data (Estimated)

maximum speed	4,800 kilometres per hour (3,000 m.p.h.)
ceiling	32,000 metres (105,000 ft.)
range	1,600 kilometres (1,000 mi.)

MODEL PV 704

At the first review meeting held at Wright-Patterson Air Force Base on November 4, 1955, Avro Canada proposed a concurrent design that would be funded by the company. As Project 1794 test results proved favourable, the new program, known as Avro PV (Private Venture) 704, was initially based on a ducted-fan ramjet powerplant and went through a series of engine changes before a finalized six-engined Armstrong-Siddeley Viper Mk. 8 configuration was proposed. Investment would involve $4–5 million to complete research, construction and flight testing of a prototype aircraft. The intention of the program was to eliminate any time delays in regards to development of Project 1794, to allow for the development of propulsion and control-system test rigs and to show a company commitment to the VTOL concept.

PV 704 specifications:

Dimensions

diameter	original configuration— 10.74 metres (35.25 ft.)
	alternate configuration— 25.24 metres (50 ft.)
height	original configuration— 2.34 metres (7.7 ft.)
	alternate configuration— 1.88 metres (6.2 ft.)

Weight

basic	6,200 kilograms (13,750 lbs.)

gross	9,000 kilograms (20,000 lbs.)
maximum	12,393 kilograms (27,322 lbs.)
Crew	original configuration— one pilot in a central circular cockpit
	alternate configuration— one pilot, one crew member in separate cockpits on each side of the central rotor
Engine Power	six Armstrong-Siddeley Viper 8 engines at 1,900 kilograms (4,188 lbs.)
Armament	alternate configuration— six missiles mounted internally

Performance Data (estimated)

maximum speed	Version 1— 579 kilometres per hour (360 m.p.h.)
	Version 2—with afterburning 2,100 kilometres per hour (1,305 m.p.h.)
ceiling	Version 1— 6,000 metres (20,000 ft.)
	Version 2—with afterburning 25,980 metres (85,000 ft.)
range	Version 1— 643 kilometres (400 mi.)
	Version 2—with afterburning 1,255 kilometres (700 mi.)

SIX-ENGINE VIPER TEST RIG

With agreement from the USAF, development commenced in January 1956 on a subsonic and supersonic PV 704 model. A full-scale test rig consisting of a complete aircraft centre section with six Viper engines, fuel cells and a Lungström compressor was completed by mid-October 1956.

The Project P.V. 704 was powered by a six Viper engine arrangement. The design was tested in a special engine test rig that approximated the flight vehicle with all of its engine systems. After tests were run, a plan was circulated to turn this rig into a hovering device much like the Rolls-Royce Flying Bedstead.

c. 1957 / Avro Aircraft Ltd

The "captive saucer" was built into a small concrete building at the back of the Shcaffcr building at Malton. Tests of this rig were in progress in 1956 and proceeded through one engine, two engine and three engines running at low power settings.

To some observers, the test rig was a frightening sight, as three fires had occurred during testing. As Wheelband commented, "It got pretty hairy. I remember John Frost building a quarter-inch steel plate, if you like, bullet-proof wall with little windows in it so that we could view the thing. Everyone was scared to death." And a nearly catastrophic incident occurred during the test runs. As it was started, a Viper engine shot out a 5-metre (16 ft.) flame, when oil that had dripped from the lower main bearing-shaft seal was ignited by the jet exhaust. Technician Bob Johnson remembered that "the engine speed increased and all efforts to stop it with engine controls failed. In other words, the engine ran wild. It picked up RPM and the whine grew louder and louder, until John Frost ordered the crew to run for safety. Led by the firemen, they ran around the Shaeffer Building to wait for the explosion. Suddenly, the engine slowed down and gradually it stopped. The whole crew waited until they had made sure it had stopped and then they peered around the end of the building, just in time to see

A completed wing section of the PV 704 Viper engine test rig shows the rib structure.

c. 1957 / via Les Wilkinson

Artist's conception of the Project 1794 also appeared later as Avro Project P.V. 704 using the exact same design (and even the same illustration).   c. 1957 / Avro Aircraft Ltd.

one of the engineers walking out of the small cement building. He had run into the building to manually shut off the fuel-supply valve to the engine. In appreciation, they made a large eighteen-inch diameter 'Hero' button and presented it to this engineer. John Frost did the presentation and then all the crew made him wear it across his chest for the full day. This was his reward." That was the end for the test rig, as Frost called a halt to its use for further testing.

The U.S. Air Force negotiated with Avro Aircraft and approved on April 30, 1957, a supplemental agreement to their basic contract to build a flying prototype of the model PV 704. This agreement extended the original contract to include additional testing to investigate the capabilities of the aircraft and evaluate its use as a weapon system. The work scheduled for this contract was to be completed by October 1958. As testing on the engine rig at Avro was over, Frost considered modifying the engine stand into a test vehicle for hovering and limited flight, although this proposal was discarded due to the risks inherent in this arrangement. The projected first flight of the PV 704 prototype was also reconsidered, and early 1959 was thought to be a more realistic time frame.

WEAPON SYSTEM 606A

On March 27, 1957, the USAF showed its continued interest in the program by extending Project 1794 through October 1958. The project name, which was later designated System 453L, now changed to Research System 606A, and the contract was to be worth $1,600,000. Avro had provided $2,500,000 up to March 1958, while the USAF had contributed $785,000 in 1954 and now $1,815,000 in 1955.

Under the highly classified program now designated Weapon System 606A, Avro developed a concept for a 24.34-metre-diameter (80 ft.), circular-winged GETOL (ground effect takeoff and landing) aircraft. Performance estimates included a top speed of 1,600 kilometres per hour (1,000 m.p.h.), and the first test flight for a prototype aircraft was slated for March 1964. Avro now redesigned Project Y2 into a six-engine Viper configuration to meet this requirement. Considering it would be years before a fighter without GETOL capabilities went that fast, this was a radical proposition.

The new contract included further studies

in the subsonic wind tunnel, development of the combustion system for supersonic flight, and studies involving operational considerations. Approximately 1,000 hours of wind-tunnel and ground-cushion tests had been completed, using upwards of seventy-five models by Avro Canada. As well, testing had begun on the propulsion system. The program director, Lt. Col. Walter P. Mairsperger, reviewed the project years later and said, "It was the promise of the Frost design that kept it alive as long as it was.... I thought the concept worth pursuing. To the end."

To others, there was no doubt that it was Frost who was the most intriguing part of the project. "The very fact that he managed to sell it says a great deal for the man. He was quite a visionary," said engineer John Conway. Bill Lamar also recalled a typical incident. "Jack Frost was a very ingenious guy. The rotors, compressors, were about fifteen feet in diameter on the vehicle we were looking at (the Avro PV 704 6 Viper Engine Test Rig) for an SAB meeting coming up. To a question someone had posed, to our great surprise, he had worked like the devil over the weekend to make this little machine. He had a hand-welded rotor and engine made up to show us, and then he was going to demonstrate it to the Scientific Advisory Board. All of a sudden, he started up the engine and the thing began whirling around the room at very high speed. I got behind the biggest guy I could find and yelled at Frost to shut the device off. After that, he got directions from me not to do anything like that again. It was basically a hand grenade flying over our heads. If it had let go, we'd all have been shredded, but that was what he was like. I thought it was very interesting to work with him."

Left: Drawing of Weapons System 606A fighter/bomber with forward-positioned cockpit and ramjets. c. 1958 / Avro Aircraft Ltd.

Right: Drawing of Weapons System 606A fighter/bomber with single air intake. c. 1958 / Avro Aircraft Ltd.

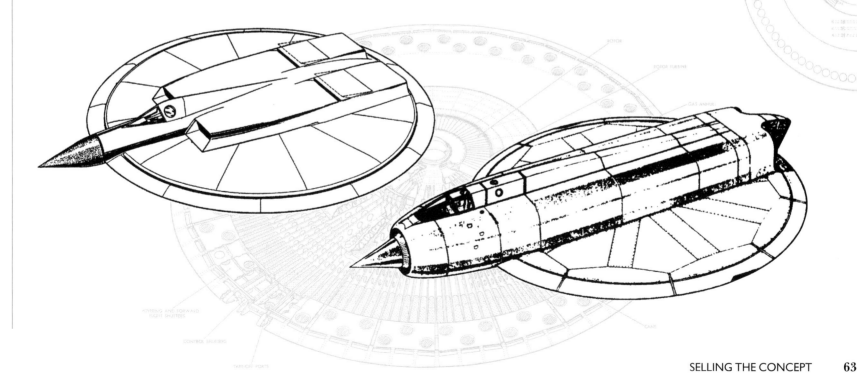

Weapon Systems 606A specifications:

Dimensions

diameter	10.74 metres (35.25 ft.)
height	2.34 metres (7.7 ft.)
wing area	configuration A— 330 metres^2 (1,083 ft.^{2})
	configuration B— 332 metres^2 (1,090 ft.^{2})

Undercarriage — nose gear and main gear of four-wheel bogie type

Weight — empty 20,000 kilograms (44,000 lbs.)

Configuration A— maximum 29,500 kilograms (65,000 lbs.)

Configuration B— maximum 20,400 kilograms (45,000 lbs.)

Crew — one pilot, one crew member

Avionics — General Electric Bantam fire-control system modified with CNI sub-system

Escape System — seat and crew ejection system

Armament — 907-kilogram (2,000 lb.) missiles plus external racks and launchers

Engine Power — two Pratt and Whitney J58 (JT11-B2-J58)

non-afterburning engines at 20,865 kilograms (46,000 lbs.)

or two General Electric J93 (J193) at 25,000 kilograms (55,000 lbs.)

Performance Data (Estimated)

maximum speed	2,400 kilometres per hour (1,500 m.p.h.)
ceiling	Version 1— 6,000 metre (20,000 ft.)
	Version 2—with afterburning 25,980 metres (85,000 ft.)
range	Version 1— 643 kilometres (400 mi.)
	Version 2—with afterburning 1,255 kilometres (700 mi.)

UNITED STATES ARMY INTEREST

On September 26 and 27, 1957, members of the U.S. Army, led by Lt. Gen. Arthur G. Trudeau, chief of research and development, visited Avro Canada. The army required a tactical craft that would give soldiers in the field greater mobility and was interested in vehicles that could hug the ground—as Project Y2 could in ground-cushion mode. Development contracts totaling $1,700,000 had been given to various companies, including Chrysler, Aerophysics, Goodyear, Piasecki, and Hiller, but the U.S. Army was not happy with any of the designs and hoped that Avro Canada could provide the needed vehicle.

AIR JEEPS

Of the many concepts in aviation that were promoted in the 1950s and 1960s, before cost and inertia reduced the willingness to take risks, one of the most promising was the "flying platform" and the related "flying jeep" that were being developed in the United States and elsewhere. These were small rotary-wing aircraft, mostly based on ducted props. The flying platforms carried a single soldier and seemed attractive for scouting missions, while the larger flying jeeps were potentially useful for a number of different military purposes. And although the flying platforms and jeeps had some advantages, they were not successful. However, the current interest in unmanned aerial vehicles (UAVs) has revived the concept as a scout platform, but in a smaller format, using cameras and sensors instead of a soldier to obtain battlefield information.

Flying platforms in the United States grew out of research on the feasibility of one-man flying platforms for combat use, conducted by the National Advisory Committee on Aeronautics in the early 1950s. The tests involved pilots flying tethered platforms, at first driven by compressed air, and then by propellers. The results showed that a pilot could control such a platform surprisingly easily through normal balancing efforts. The NACA results were released to the public and resulted in three efforts by Hiller, Benson and de Lackner to build flying platforms.

In the mid-1950s, the de Lackner company produced a pair of platform vehicles, the DH-4 Helivector and the DH-5 Aerocycle. The de Lackner machines consisted of a frame with skids or floats and a 40-horsepower Mercury outboard motor. The motor drove a pair of 4.6-metre (15 ft.) contra-rotating rotors directly above the frame, while the pilot stood vertically on a platform above the rotors, using motorcycle handlebars and a twist-grip throttle for control. The de Lackner machines could fly at up to 105 kilometres per hour (65 m.p.h.), carry up to 55 kilograms (121 lbs.) payload besides the pilot, and fly for an hour. The Bensen B-10 Propcopter powered by a 72-horsepower McCulloch engine, consisted of a frame with 1.2-metre (3.94 ft.) props mounted vertically on the front and back. It flew in 1959 but apparently was difficult to handle. Both the de Lackner and Bensen projects were ultimately abandoned by their companies.

The Hiller designs were better thought out and attracted much public attention. Hiller developed their first flying platform on the basis of a contract from the Office of Naval Research (ONR) for a one-man flying platform. The result was the VZ-1 Pawnee, which featured a pair of contra-rotating propellers spinning inside a duct with a diameter of 1.5 metres (5 ft.), with each propeller driven by its own 44-horsepower, two-stroke engine. The duct improved lift and reduced the likelihood of ground accidents.

The pilot stood above the duct, surrounded by a circular handrail, and could control the engines with a twist-grip throttle.

Hiller followed the VZ-1 with a similar but larger flying platform, the VZ-1E, for a U.S. Army contract. The VZ-1E had three engines, driving propellers in a 2.4-metre (8 ft.) diameter duct. This more than doubled the disc area, increasing payload and range while reducing noise and downdraft. Hiller also built a version of the VZ-1 with a deeper, barrel-like duct that improved lift performance and allowed the machine to carry heavier payloads. The Hiller machines seemed to have merits, but they were powered by small piston engines. The arrival of small turbine engines suggested that more ambitious things could be done along the same lines, and so were born the flying jeeps. Officially, the concept of the flying jeeps was the result of a late-1950s requirement by the U.S. Army Transportation Research Command to develop tactical VTOL aircraft in the one- to two-tonne range.

The first of the breed was the Piasecki 59H Airgeep, which was given the U.S. Army designation VZ-8P. The Airgeep was 7.9 metres (26 ft.) long and 2.7 metres (8.85 ft.) wide, with three-bladed rotors in ducts in the front and the back. The pilot and passenger sat between the ducts. In this initial Airgeep, the 2.4-metre-diameter (7.9 ft.) rotors were driven by a pair of 180-horsepower Lycoming piston engines, later replaced by a single 425-horsepower Turbomeca Artouste IIB turbine engine.

The rotors spun in opposite directions. Control was provided by varying rotor pitch (as well as with vanes in the downdraft). Forward motion was achieved by pitching the aircraft forward. The Airgeep was put through trials for both the U.S. Army and Navy over the next few years. The engine was upgraded again to an AiResearch 331-6, which had a higher power-to-weight ratio. For navy trials, which began in June 1961, the floats were fitted, and the aircraft was designated the PA-59 SeaGeep.

Piasecki wanted to build a larger and more efficient Airgeep, and the Army Transportation Research Command obliged them by issuing a contract for what Piasecki called the Model 59K and what the army called the VZ-8P(B) AirGeep II. It was similar to the Airgeep, except that the aircraft was bent in the middle so that the rotors were tilted fore and aft, reducing drag in forward flight. The AirGeep II used twin 400-horsepower Turbomeca Artouste IIC turboshaft engines, linked so that if one failed the other would drive both rotors. One engine could also be linked to the landing wheels to drive the machine around on the ground. The increased power allowed a maximum takeoff weight of 2.2 tonnes.

The army also pursued a "flying truck" in parallel with the flying jeeps, though the flying truck didn't get as much press. Curtiss-Wright Corporation developed this machine under the designation VZ-7AP. It was a simple beam with a pilot up front and four horizontal propellers at each of four corners; the props

Project 1794 scale full-plane wind-tunnel model used for supersonic testing at MIT Laboratory. The mount is "stinger" or rear-mounted.

1956 / Avro Aircraft Ltd.

were all driven by a single 425-horsepower Turbomeca Artouste engine, mounted underneath the central beam. Differential pitch between the propellers and a rudder in the turbine exhaust provided control for the aircraft. The flying truck was 5.2 metres (17 ft.) long and 4.9 metres (16 ft.) wide and weighed 770 kilograms (1,698 lbs.), with 250 kilograms (551 lbs.) of that payload. The VZ-7 was tested in 1959 and 1960 but nothing came of the project.

The most radical approach to providing aerial mobility to soldiers was the later Bell Jet Flying Belt, or Aerospace Jet Belt, that was developed in 1969 under a $3-million contract sponsored by the United States Department of Defense's Advanced Research Projects Agency (ARPA). A 195-kilogram (430 lb.) Williams Research Corporation WR-19 high-bypass twin-spool turbojet powered the lifting device.

The operator strapped the 56-kilogram (124 lb.) jet pack on and powered straight up.

Flight control was achieved through manually actuated hand controls and arm motions, giving the operator complete freedom of flight, including vertical axis rotation and hovering manoeuvres. Range and flight duration of the Jet Belt would be measured in miles and minutes, instead of the feet and seconds to which flights of rocket-powered predecessors had been limited. Like earlier rocket-powered devices, performance was limited by the relatively small fuel supply, but speeds of 48 kilometres per hour (30 m.p.h.) and altitudes of 13 metres (45 ft.) were achieved. On January 26, 1970, Bell Aircraft granted a license to manufacture, use and sell certain small-lift device systems, including the Jet Flying Belt, to the Williams Research Corporation, Walled Lake, Michigan.

The flying platforms and flying jeeps had some merits; they were smaller than helicopters, and could operate in ground cover more successfully. However, helicopters could land more easily on rough terrain and had more convenient seating arrangements. Most critical, the flying platforms and jeeps had much smaller rotors, and were inefficient in fuel management. There were also apparently concerns about the practicality of the one-person flying platforms, since they provided relatively little capability in relationship to larger rotary-winged aircraft, while still presenting nearly the same support problems. In short, they didn't have sufficient advantages over helicopters to make them worth further development.

Throughout 1957, the Avro Canada Special Projects Group, led by Frost, made a series of presentations to the U.S. military and the Canadian Army concerning a smaller, subsonic version of its VTOL project. The craft, named the "Avromobile," was featured in a report entitled "U.S. Army Requirement for a New Family of Air Vehicles," dated November 26, 1957. Avro personnel were then invited to brief Gen. Herbert J. Gavin, chief of the Weapons Phasing Division, at a meeting in the Pentagon on November 29, 1957. What Avro proposed was a vehicle based on the PV 704 design. The U.S. Army would arrange funding to procure two vehicles for completion of the full test program. The value of the joint USAF/U.S. Army contracts for fabrication and testing of the prototype vehicles was set at $4,432,497.

On January 29, 1958, the Special Projects Group met with Dr. Alexander Lippisch, the foremost wartime German aeronautical expert, who then resided in the United States. Lippisch had devoted his energy in the postwar era to ground-effect research and had designed an unusual aircraft, the Collins Aerodyne. It was 10 metres (32.8 ft.) long by 4 metres (13 ft.) wide and powered by two 225-brake-horsepower Lycoming reciprocating engines. The Aerodyne was not only expected to have VTOL capability but also an optimal cruise speed of 300 kilometres per hour (186 m.p.h.). Although the Special Projects Group did not go much further in

collaborating with Lippisch, he offered to loan Avro some movies on the Aerodyne design.

By April 1958, the USAF, the U.S. Army, and the U.S. Office of the Secretary of Defense had agreed to establish an integrated USAF/U.S. Army program with joint funding but under the management of the Air Force. The program would satisfy the army subsonic requirement and be a first step towards realizing the supersonic USAF flying saucer. It was agreed that the supersonic USAF Weapons System 606A and Avro PV 704 programs would be reoriented to study the simpler, subsonic U.S. Army vehicle. Avro ended the PV 704 project at this point, abandoning the test rig it had already built. The new design would be completed first as a research vehicle for the concurrent USAF supersonic-fighter programs and to satisfy the U.S. Army requirement for a flying jeep. Thus, the Avromobile—later more popularly known as the Avrocar—was born.

CHAPTER EIGHT

THE AVROCAR

ALTHOUGH UNKNOWN to most Avro employees, a secret program known derisively as the "saucer" project by some senior staff in Avro Canada, continued to be funded by the American military throughout the 1950s. As reported by Williams in the *Winnipeg Tribune* in 1976, "Among those who were in the know, there was great conflict. Some thought Frost was loony and the company people who were ready to put some cash into it were even loonier."

The supersonic fighter development Weapons Systems 606A continued to dominate Frost's research. A USAF proposal for a tactical fighter/bomber, SR-198, dated January 26, 1959, laid out the specifications for an advanced Mach-3 weapons system. Williams noted that "the main problem with the designs that were proposed was in the propulsion system. A very large jet engine with thrust in the range of 4,535 kilograms (10,000 lbs.) or more was needed.... Because of the circular shape and the basic concept of a machine that would takeoff and land vertically and slowly, its power or thrust had to be exerted around the periphery of the disc.... It posed a seemingly impossible problem. It was unheard of. Those who thought Frost was out of his mind figured he was stumped now. But not John. He came up with a design that defied all previous technology. Had there been enough time and money, it is conceivable his revolutionary engine could have been built."

Before committing to this design, Frost worked on a proof-of-concept subsonic vehicle that would result in the Avrocar. "Building the saucers was not that great a problem," wrote Williams. "Conventional aircraft construction was used. The outer skin was aluminum as in ordinary airplanes. But the powerplant was something else. Frost's design...was purely experimental, an attempt to prove his theory. It had great potential." A two-section wooden mockup of the Avrocar was built as well in 1958, and served to provide confirmation of dimensions and fittings as well as a visual reference for production planners.

AVROCAR TIMELINE

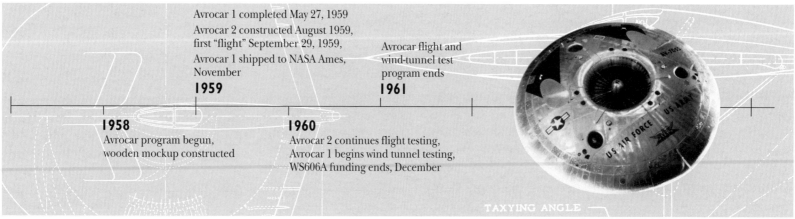

Avrocar 1 completed May 27, 1959
Avrocar 2 constructed August 1959, first "flight" September 29, 1959,
Avrocar 1 shipped to NASA Ames, November

1959

Avrocar flight and wind-tunnel test program ends

1961

1958
Avrocar program begun, wooden mockup constructed

1960
Avrocar 2 continues flight testing, Avrocar 1 begins wind tunnel testing, WS606A funding ends, December

TAXYING ANGLE

Under a new USAF contract, AF33 (600)-3796, the Avro Canada VZ-9-AV Avrocar (sometimes referred to as the Avrocar 1 or Model 1 in company documents) was built primarily as a scaled-down 5.4-metre-diameter (18 ft.) research vehicle. The more usual designation VZ-9-AV referred to the VTOL experimental ninth vehicle; the AV stood for the contractor, Avro Canada, and the designations VZ-9AV, VZ-9, VZ-9V or VZ-9A were sometimes used in error or for the sake of convenience.

A pilot on the port side and an observer on the starboard side sat in separate cockpits, facing forward. For later developments to meet U.S. Army requirements, changes were anticipated in the pilot and aircrew locations. The Avrocar was powered by three Continental J-69 (licence-built Turbomeca Marboré) turbojets, turning a central impeller (turborotor) built by Orenda Engines to launch it airborne with downward thrust. The blades of the Avrocar turborotor were hollow, with internal reinforcing, and brazed to cement the parts. Testing of the first turborotor was conducted for 150 hours without mishap. The aircraft utilized a peripheral-thrust system of vanes and shutters to propel the craft at an expected airspeed of nearly 500 kilometres per hour (300 m.p.h.), with a maximum range of 1,600 kilometres (995 mi.). Directional control also came from the vane/shutter system that allowed the pilot to move in any direction. The Avrocar used three small, double-bogie wheels and later tricycle landing pads for an undercarriage. The entire package was enclosed in a circular disc shape that had the appearance of a lenticular body.

Avrocar VZ-9-AV specifications:

Dimensions

diameter	5.486 metres (18 ft.)
height	2.34 metres (7.7 ft.)
wing area	77.4 metres^2 (254 ft.^{2})

Undercarriage	nose gear and main gear of two-wheel bogie type, landing pads later fitted
Weight	empty—1,360 kilograms (3,000 lbs.)
	maximum—2,563 kilograms (5,650 lbs.)
Crew	one pilot one crew member(observer)
Engine Power	three Continental J69-T-9 non-afterburning engines at 421 kilograms (927 lbs.)

Performance Data (Estimated)

maximum speed	482 kilometres per hour (300 m.p.h.)
range	127 kilometres (79 mi.)

According to Williams's 1976 article, "Besides aerodynamic efficiency, there was another important reason for the circular air shape. To accommodate bigger and faster jets, commercial and military, we have had to build bigger airports and longer runways. A saucer-plane would take off and land vertically like a helicopter. No need for runways at all. Considering the problems associated with huge airports, the prospect of virtually no runways at all is compelling. Then there is the implication for the military. Armies have been looking for a vehicle that will give a soldier more mobility than a jeep or personnel carrier—something that is not earthbound, that can go anywhere, up, down, sideways, backwards, forwards. The saucer-machine held out this promise. That's why the Canadian Army and U.S. Army were the strongest supporters of the Avro saucer."

However, regardless of the U.S. Army funding that fueled the project, Frost and the project team continued to work on the supersonic fighter program, Weapons Systems 606A, in a trade-off arrangement that saw six weeks of work on the Avrocar and then a switch to the fighter project.

WASHINGTON REVEALS THE AVROCAR PROJECT

As reported in the *Financial Post*, April 1959, the existence of the Avrocar project was made public at the U.S. Congress Space Committee hearings that month. The Pentagon witnesses, including Research and Engineering Deputy Director John B. Macauley, indicated that the saucer project would not involve an outer-space craft. "It would skim

the Earth's surface or fly at altitudes reached by conventional aircraft," said Macauley. According to sources in Washington, the big advantage would be a vehicle with helicopter-like performance, but capable of much greater speeds. A flying disc also offered the tantalizing prospect of near "invisibility" to radar. Stealth has brought a whole new set of parameters to aircraft design. Although the techniques for foiling radar are complex and largely classified, a key principle is to minimize the surfaces that might intersect a radar beam at a right angle. The flying disc seemed to offer that potential.

Creating a weapon system that had sophisticated features and was able to carry out low-flying missions while escaping detection by radar was intriguing to Congress. One congressional source noted in an article in the *Financial Post* that there was concern that the U.S. Air Force (only one of the funding bodies, however) was not moving fast enough on the project, and that it had not been heavily funded.

The Canadian military maintained a presence throughout the Avrocar/WS 606A programs, but no commitment was ever made to become a partner in the program. Avro Canada continued to lobby for RCAF funding for Weapons System 606A, and ultimately it was able to interest the Canadian

Overleaf: Avrocar evaluated in the wind tunnel in the NASA Ames Research Centre.

military in a proposal to satisfy the Canadian OCH 85 Attack/Strike Weapons System requirement. However, the RCAF and Canadian Army involvement in the Avro Canada VTOL program remained limited to participation in meetings with Avro Canada and the joint USAF/U.S. Army project teams.

BLACK FRIDAY

In the midst of production, the Avrocar was hit hard by the Canadian government cancellation of the Avro CF-105 Arrow on "Black Friday," February 20, 1959. All A. V. Roe Canada employees except executive management were laid off immediately, and it was three days before members of the Special Projects Group were reinstated. The Americans therefore inserted a stop/go-ahead decision date of March 4, 1959, into the Avrocar schedule and halted the construction of the second prototype.

While losing some key members of his team, Frost was back at work. Avro Canada now tried to take a direct hand in the operations of the Special Projects Group, initially by reassigning Avro Arrow project personnel to Frost. A decision was also made by the executive management that the Avrocar/WS 606A project would be actively supported, for as noted by Lt. Col. James Hall and Capt. Daniel Murray in a 1959 trip report, the USAF/U.S. Army programs were "all Avro has."

Avrocar S/N 58-7055, the first of two planned prototype aircraft, officially designated U.S. Army VZ-9-AV and identified as

AV-7055 (featuring both U.S. Army and USAF markings), was completed and rolled out on May 27, 1959. The original plan was to build four units made up of three main pie-shaped sections, but only two were actually assembled, although spares were sufficient to make at least one additional machine. Avro Canada offered to use its own funds to complete the third vehicle, referred to as Avro PV 705 or 707, but reciprocal arrangements with the USAF for engine acquisition fell through, and the third vehicle was never constructed.

With the problems that the contractor was facing in the wake of the cancellation by the Canadian government of its premier fighter program, the Avro Arrow, the American military now imposed a new go/no-go date of April 30, 1959, for the Avrocar project. A deadline date of April 1960 was also instituted for Weapons Systems 606A to proceed to further stages. At that point, a technical evaluation of the Avrocar flight-test program and pre-phase 1 report of WS 606A would decide the fate of the supersonic project.

Two hundred engineering personnel were rehired for the CF-100 and Avrocar programs on March 16, 1959. The most senior staff, however, bumped junior personnel, and many newcomers were assigned to the Special Projects Group. This resulted in what Al Wheelband later described as a "great hiccup," as project engineers who had worked for years in the CF-100 or CF-105 program had to learn where they fit in on the VTOL project.

Avrocar evaluated at maximum height in the 12-metre-by-24-metre (40 x 80 ft.) wind tunnel in the NASA Ames Research Centre.

c. 1960 / NASA Ames Research Center

When Frost, as the Avro Canada chief designer (VTOL) and head of the Special Projects Group, was able to show that Avro Canada could continue the program under a reconfigured project team, the joint U.S. Army/USAF program was given a go-ahead in May 1959. The U.S. Air Force had a continuing interest in the supersonic fighter program, and USAF Letter Contract AF33(600)-39722, dated June 30, 1959, included an additional $600,000 for VTOL studies of the WS 606A supersonic fighter. In July, Avro Canada inquired of the USAF if a newly proposed Avro private-venture program, funded at $1.5 million, could be used to supplement the WS 606A effort. If approved, the company would enlarge the Special Projects Group to accommodate the new project. But the USAF made no commitment to an enlarged program.

Under Supplemental Agreement Number 1 of the contract, the second Avrocar (called the Mark 2 presumably to indicate the second prototype), 59-4975, was authorized and was rolled out in August 1959. To assist in the flight-test program, a flight simulator was also developed by Avro. The simulator, comprised of a representative cockpit complete with all flying controls and instrumentation, was pneumatically controlled by an analog computer system.

By October 1959, trade-off studies that continued the USAF requirement for Weapon Systems 606A began to take a new direction, as Avro Canada now made proposals that completely altered the original VTOL concept. Encouraged by the approval of the WS 606A Pre-Phase 1 Planning Report on November 18, 1959, a radically different concept was being considered by the newcomers in the WS606A Design Office. As Wheelband commented in an 1983 interview, "The effect on the design group was pretty catastrophic. Here we were working for several years, and watched this thing develop in its finest detail only to be shown up by a bunch of guys...all conventional thinkers who immediately started thinking conventionally about the thing and trying to make it into an airplane as they knew airplanes.... They really compromised the whole design."

Thomas G. Higgins, the new project engineer of the 606A team, proposed a high-sweep delta configuration that no longer utilized the peripheral jet. Like many of the new members of the Special Projects Group, Higgins had been associated with the CF-100 as project engineer and the CF-105 Arrow Mk. 1 as acting project designer.

The American military representatives were evidently caught off guard by the new proposal, and after consultation with Lt. Col. J. N. Hall at headquarters, ARDC Wright-Patterson Air Force Base directed the WS 606A team to continue with the design of the circular planform. Avro Canada argued that the new proposal fit the original requirements and persuaded the U.S. to at least consider the new configuration. It was becoming evident that Avro Canada was lobbying desperately for its future survival. Meanwhile, Frost took a more direct role in the flight-test program of the Avrocar and virtually dropped out of the supersonic fighter program.

Avrocar 1 evaluated in the wind tunnel in the NASA Ames Research Centre.

c. 1960 / NASA Ames Research Center

NASA Ames technician checking the Avrocar in the wind tunnel. Note the angle at which the craft is positioned; the Avrocar could be evaluated at various orientations through hinged supports. c.1960 / NASA Ames Research Center

Opposite Page: The Avrocar was modified at the NASA Ames Research Center to evaluate the efficiency or potential of a tail unit. The T-tail was not effective in improving stability and was removed. c.1960 / NASA Ames Research Center

TESTING

Rare film footage exists of the Avrocar project, including design and construction of both vehicles, wind-tunnel tests, and many of the tethered and free-flight tests. Between June 9 and October 7, 1959, the first Avrocar underwent a thirty-two-hour static rig test at Avro in Malton, in a specially built rig developed by Orenda. The unmanned aircraft was suspended approximately 1.828 metres (6 ft.) above the ground during these tests. In the forty-four tests conducted, it was evident that turborotor performance was not optimum. Approximately a third of the thrust was lost due to turbine exhaust inefficiencies. Cold and hot air mixing in the duct structure could only be redirected properly with a complete redesign of the exhaust area.

With the design of the Avrocar advanced to the production stage, any structural changes would require a complete redesign. The project team made a decision to keep the original structure and limit the flight testing to the ground-cushion environment. On reflection, this was a costly decision that was to cripple the entire program. Excessive temperatures from the buried engines were also encountered, plaguing the static and flight tests throughout the program. Observers constantly remarked on the shrieking engine noise and the blisteringly hot cockpit temperatures, which at times caused the instruments to be burned brown.

On November 21, 1959, Avro Canada shipped the first vehicle to the United States in a specially constructed wooden crate. It first travelled by barge across Lake Ontario and then by a tug that took it as far as New York City. The prototype was subsequently offloaded to a U.S. Navy ship that sailed through the Panama Canal to the NASA Ames Wind Tunnel in California for full-scale wind-tunnel tests commencing in April 1960. The wind-tunnel tests were to simulate not only hover conditions but also free flight, as the Avrocar could be mounted in the 12-by-24-metre (40 x 80 ft.) wind tunnel at heights up to 3.85 metres (12.66 ft.). A second round of wind-tunnel testing commenced in April 1961.

After five months of dealing with the thermodynamic problems and deficiencies that were encountered in the static testing, the

first tethered flight test with Spud Potocki, Avro company test pilot, was conducted on the second vehicle (which did not have canopies fitted to aid in air circulation), on September 29, 1959. He wore a specially designed lightweight flight suit that protected him from the heat of the cockpit. Flights were often conducted in cool weather to aid in keeping cockpit temperatures at a reasonable level. Safety concerns were addressed by the provision of small roll-over bars and fire extinguishers, but "Potocki proved that ejection seats were not required, by shutting down all three engines, and unbuckling his seat harness and leaping from the vehicle in 0.6 seconds!" says Ron Page.

Avrocar 1 was continually modified at the NASA Ames Research Center in order to correspond with the alterations made to the flying test model in Canada. c. 1960 / NASA Ames Research Center

The first tethers were based on lengths of cable anchored to rings in the concrete surface of the flight-test area. With the tugging of the Avrocar on one length of cable, an unstable pitching movement resulted. When the cables were weighted instead, the pilot could counter oscillations more effectively, and the vehicle was also able to move more precisely. Tests continued throughout 1959, with the first free flight conducted on December 5, 1959.

Potocki entered his comments on the initial series of tests in the flight log. "With a quarter lift control application, the vehicle became airborne at 83% engine rpm. with half fuel. On first unstick, it became obvious that the behaviour of the vehicle was more conventional than at any time before. The getaway from the ground was clean and rather steady, requiring only small control movement by the pilot...the aircraft was definitely stabilized this time within the ground cushion, the stabilizing action of the gyro being felt quite clearly through small amplitude oscillations which were present at all times. At the one-quarter left control setting, there was still much liveliness in the system whenever any larger correction to attitude was made by the pilot. This effect seemed to stir up the oscillatory response 'hubcapping.' The control in hovering flight was adequate in both pitch and roll."

The Avrocar was able to clear small obstacles without difficulty, but maximum altitude was never more than about one metre

Avrocar 1 was evaluated at the maximum height of the NASA Ames wind tunnel.

c. 1960 / NASA Ames Research Center

The wind-tunnel testing of the Avrocar revealed a lack of power and inadequate control forces.

c. 1960 / NASA Ames Research Center

although some observers said it flew as high as three metres on a tether. The Avrocar was able to hover but it didn't fly above the maximum height that could be attained with the air cushion, except in a tethered flight. At that point, the aircraft would be in the free-flying mode, theoretically able to fly in any direction. Unfortunately, it never did. Its ability to rise, hover and fly at top speed was extremely disappointing, mostly due to thrust dissipation in the impeller. But the matter of control in free flight was its undoing.

"Frost knew, in advance, that he had not solved the control problem but he flew it anyway—or tried to," using the natural gyroscopic control of the rotor to augment the stabilization system of ducts, vanes and spoilers, noted Williams in 1976. "A conventional aircraft is controlled by the tail fin and rudder and the stabilizers. The saucer had nothing. Frost's idea was to maintain control by manipulating vanes mounted around the periphery of the saucer. To take off vertically, the vanes would be positioned so that the jet thrust was directed downward all around the craft. To go forward, the front vanes would be closed, directing all the power through the rear vents. And so with sideways movement. The variable vanes were controlled by the pilot with a control column much as in a conventional aircraft. The trouble was, the system didn't work. No matter what Frost did, he couldn't solve the problem. The project was in jeopardy after flight stability problems could not be overcome."

On March 15, 1960, Fred J. Drinkwater III, a NASA Ames research engineer and test pilot, carried out a number of tethered and free flights at the Avro test facilities at Malton with the second prototype. He observed that at below the critical height of approximately one metre (three feet), the Avrocar was able to attain "forward and side velocities of approximately twenty miles per hour and 'quick stops' from these speeds were accomplished easily. Horizontal accelerations are obtained by inclining the vehicle in the desired direction as with a helicopter. Height control did not require attention because of the very stable variation of thrust with height. The overall hovering handling qualities of the Avrocar are satisfactory in ground effect. It has positive stability in pitch, roll and height."

As Potocki had found, once the critical height had been reached, Drinkwater noted "an abrupt change in stability as it is an abrupt loss in lift in one quadrant of the disc. The affected quadrant drops abruptly but it recovers lift before striking the ground." This was the same dipping and twisting motion observed by others and referred to by some Avro engineers as "hubcapping." (Imagine a hubcap being thrown, and you see a twirling frisbee-like flight and a bouncing motion as it settles to the ground.) However, Drinkwater was not deterred by the slow progress of the Avrocar program, saying, "All the new flying concepts are cans of worms at the early stage."

In 1961 Maj. Walter J. Hodgson, the USAF project pilot, flew the second Avrocar with a focussing ring-control modification through its last series of flight tests at Malton. His observations were contained in a report entitled "Avrocar Flight Evaluation," dated January 1962. "The aircraft is controllable at heights between 1 and 1½ feet (distance from bottom of the wheels to the ground). Critical height in present configuration is about 2 ft which is approximately 6 inches lower than that obtained during the first evaluation.... The maximum airspeed that could be obtained during the first evaluation was 25–30 knots.... A slightly higher airspeed can be obtained in calm air, however a slight gust will cause the aircraft to pitch up...."

The aircraft managed to clear a shallow ditch during rough field trials, but generally the flight characteristics were only marginal. In the recommendations made by 1st Lt. Wallace H. Deckert, the USAF project engineer and Hodgson, they focussed on the deteriorated engine and turborotor performance and lack of controllability over the speed range of the Avrocar but cautioned that modifications would only be feasible if the program were continued. The Avrocar program, however, was in great danger in 1961.

In 1961, the *Financial Post* reported that "despite the failure of the control system, the U.S. was not quite ready to give up." The American experts assigned to the project were already working closely with Frost. Williams said in 1976, "They wanted to see if they could pinpoint the saucer's control problem. The [wind tunnel] test confirmed that the control problem was, as of that date, insurmountable." Additional flight tests that concentrated on solving the stability problems were made in the period between July 1960 and June 1961, for a combined total of ninety-three test flights of approximately seventy-five hours. During the second series of tests, the peripheral nozzle was removed, as various efforts to improve the low-speed hovering and handling performance were analyzed, including the fitting of a focussing ring and movable vanes at various junctures of the fuselage. At Avro, a wooden tail fin was also fitted in late 1960 but was discarded as no benefits were realized in the area of stabilization and control. A T-tail was also fitted at the NASA Ames Wind Tunnel on the first prototype, but this modification was similarly rejected after testing.

The instability of the Avrocar stemmed from the properties of the "tree-trunk" of focussed air that was generated by the annular jet. As the vehicle was brought closer to the ground, the mass of air abruptly changed from tree-trunk shape to a curtain shape. If the vehicle tipped into the transient zone, the air jet again took the tree-trunk form, leading to a dipping and straightening action. The manual controls and mechanical devices that were intended to increase stability were simply not effective. Recent years have seen the maturation of the electronic flight controls needed to stabilize a saucer, and Avro itself made an effort to design a computer-based system similar to that used in the Avro Arrow. When American experts rejected this modified system, the decision had already been made to abandon the Avrocar project.

The saucer design still had supporters, both at Avro and at Wright Field, but a redesign of the internal duct area was necessary, which meant a nearly entirely new aircraft. Without much enthusiasm, Frost set to work on a new Avrocar. Engine and turborotor performance problems that seriously reduced the Avrocar's flight envelope would have been solved by the new design. But it was not to be.

SECTION A-A

CHAPTER NINE

THE END OF A DREAM

"IT WAS A very ingenious idea, but it was just way too early," said Col. Daniel C. Murray, who earlier had managed the program for the USAF and had flown in the Avrocar as an observer. Shortly before his death in 1999, Murray stated that helicopters and other specialized craft had taken over the roles for which the Avrocar was planned. "I'm sure you could build a flying saucer today," he had once reported. "The question is, why?" Fred J. Drinkwater III, a research engineer and NASA Ames test pilot assigned to the Avrocar project, summed up the program, saying, "Tests showed the saucer would have taken too much development effort. Other concepts proved more promising."

Murray also knew something about the Avro project that he couldn't reveal at the time. "One ominous cloud hung over the Avro program from its onset. The United States and Canadian governments were discussing Canadian cost sharing and acquisition of the U.S. Air Force F-108 supersonic fighter. During the middle of the Avrocar program, the Canadian government and the United States Air Force had reached an agreement on the F-108 project and the Avro Arrow was cancelled. It was ironic that the F-108 was also cancelled. That was a kind of deal that you [Canada] were going to get that supersonic aircraft and we decided at high altitude that the mission had gone away."

United States research scientist Bernard Lindenbaum later confirmed that the fighter program that the U.S. military had been advocating was the highly advanced North American XF-108 Rapier, which not only looked remarkably like the Arrow, but hinted at even greater performance. The XF-108 was initially intended to be an advanced long-range fighter escort of the North American XB-70 Valkyrie. Eventually, the XB-70 program was altered to that of a research effort. Both bomber and fighter projects were cancelled in the wake of the

AVROCAR / WS 606A TIMELINE

1960 Weapons System 606A cancelled, new Avro designs rejected

1961 Avrocar program cancelled after final flight testing at Malton, NASA Ames testing ends

1962 A. V. Roe Canada is dissolved de Havilland Canada absorbs facilities

1966 NASA Ames sends first Avrocar to NASM (Washington)

1968 Second Avrocar displayed in Montreal, Canada

1979 Second Avrocar is sent to U.S. Army Transportation Museum for gate guardian display

1999 NASM Avrocar earmarked for restoration and display at Dulles facility

2000 U.S. Army Transportation Museum Avrocar to be relocated inside

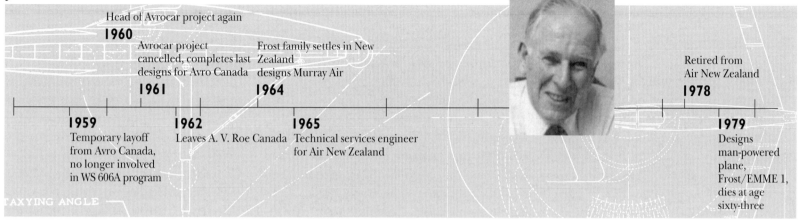

Head of Avrocar project again
1960

Avrocar project cancelled, completes last designs for Avro Canada

Frost family settles in New Zealand designs Murray Air

Retired from Air New Zealand
1978

1961

1964

1959
Temporary layoff from Avro Canada, no longer involved in WS 606A program

1962
Leaves A. V. Roe Canada

1965
Technical services engineer for Air New Zealand

1979
Designs man-powered plane, Frost/EMME 1, dies at age sixty-three

TAXYING ANGLE

reevaluation of the role of the North American XB-70.

TOM'S FOLLY

The Special Projects Group was in disarray as Avro Canada began to distance itself from Frost and the original project team. According to a trip report made by Air Research and Development Command Project Engineer John Chuprun Jr. in 1960, a decision was made to utilize "more practical engineers who worked on the Avro Arrow." Chuprun reported that Higgins, the new project engineer on Weapons System 606A, declared, "Avro does not want a circular planform for the supersonic vehicle.... Ignore all information in previous work except wind tunnel test data done by Avro on the supersonic aircraft as he does not want Avro technical competence to be judged by that information."

But the original members of the Special Projects Group chafed under the direction of the Higgins team. On a drawing of the new Configuration 1 issued by the Weapons Systems 606A team, one of them scribbled "Tom's Folly." The new vectored-thrust, delta-winged design (which incidentally looked much like the Avro Arrow) became known as Configuration 3 in the design office. Avro Canada sent a proposal based on this design to the War Office, Whitehall, England, for consideration, but was unsuccessful in gaining support. A lobby effort directed toward the Canadian government for funding was similarly rejected.

Time was running out.

Weapon Systems 606A Alternate Configuration 1 specifications:
Configuration based on a low-wing delta fighter with vectored lift-engines. The tail unit used a swept tail.

Dimensions

length	32 metres (105 ft.)
height	6.37 metres (20.9 ft.)
span	14.5 metres (47.6 ft.)
wing area	336 metres^2 (1,102 ft.^{2})
leading edge sweep	67.5 degrees with leading-edge droop
trailing-edge sweep	26 degrees
Undercarriage	nose gear and main gear of four-wheel bogie type
Weight	maximum 20,400 kilograms (45,000 lbs.)
Crew	one pilot one crew member

Performance Data (Estimated)

maximum speed	2,655 kilometres per hour (1,650 m.p.h.)

Configuration 2 specifications:
Configuration 2 was similar to Configuration 1 except for a more raked or swept wing and a single tailplane.

Configuration 3 specifications:
This configuration was based on a high-wing delta fighter with louver lift-engines. The tail unit also used a swept tail.

Dimensions

length	26.82-metre (88 ft.)
span	14.53 metres (47.66 ft.)
wing area	335.9 metres^2 (1,102 ft.^{2})
leading edge sweep	30 degrees

Weight

	empty— 20,956 kilograms (46,200 lbs.)
	gross— 30,617 kilograms (67,500 lbs.)

Engine Power

	two General Electric X369 without afterburning at 26,580 kilograms (58,600 lbs.)

Performance Data (Estimated)

maximum speed	2,400 kilometres per hour (1,500 m.p.h.)

CANCELLATION

As project director of the VZ-9-AV Avrocar, Frost and the remaining members of his team struggled with the problems of the Avrocar. He privately informed American representatives that he was tacitly no longer in charge of the Weapons Systems 606A effort, and said, as mentioned in Capt. Daniel Murray's trip report in 1960, that he considered the new designs "an abortion which had no resemblance to his own ideas and original concepts."

On July 20, 1960, the Directorate of Advanced Systems Technology, USAF, closed down Weapons System 606A, as funds had finally run out. Avro Canada continued to discuss potential project proposals that focused on lift-jet and vectored-thrust designs, but there was no American interest in pursuing these approaches.

THE AVROCAR IS CANCELLED

In December 1961, the Avrocar project was officially over, as the American development contract was completed after an expenditure of $7.5 million U.S. A number of future Avrocar developments were being considered at this time. Some designs used attached tails, elliptical wings, and revised cockpit accommodations. In late 1960, Frost had redesigned the VZ-9-AV Avrocar with a pair of J-85 turbojets, a larger turborotor of improved performance and wing extension/winglets joined to the central disc planform.

The preliminary assessment made by Wright-Patterson personnel was that the Avrocar could have been redesigned to meet its original specifications, but that the expenditure needed was too high. Although this final Avrocar proposal might have solved the VZ-9-AV's deficiencies in stabilization and performance, the U.S. military felt that the aircraft, even in a revamped form, in light of progress made in light helicopters, did not merit continued development.

At the conclusion of the program, as the vehicles were technically property of the United States, the second Avrocar was delivered in 1966 to the U.S. Army facility in Fort Eustis, Virginia, for storage. It was returned to Canada briefly in 1968 when on display at the "Man and His World" exhibit in Montreal, before being returned to Fort Eustis for eventual display at the U.S. Army Transportation Museum in 1979. The first Avrocar was retained at NASA Ames for storage, then was donated to the National Air and Space Museum in 1966.

THE AVROCAR AS A GROUND-CUSHION VEHICLE

Although the Avrocar completed all of its untethered flight-test program in ground cushion and never achieved free flight, its development as a hovercraft was not investigated fully. Using almost exactly the same propulsion setup, in the early 1960s the British SRN-1, the first hovercraft, used basically an Avrocar propulsion system with a flexible rubber skirt, which greatly improved the use of downward thrust. As reported by Williams, Frost later recalled, "It is unfortunate that our sights were set on developing a supersonic vertical takeoff aircraft when Avro stumbled on the ground cushion, otherwise we might have paid more attention to its possible uses as an amphibious surface vehicle.... We missed its potential as a method of improving the performance of water-borne craft."

In a paper presented to the Canadian Aeronautical Institute in 1961, John Frost commented on the fact that new ideas are often thought of and worked on at the same time in different parts of the world without one group having knowledge of the activities of the others. "In many cases," Frost said, "this is due to the state of the art, so that there are numbers of groups working who are all on the verge of taking the next step within the same period. In the case of the ground cushion, this was not so, since it was technically possible for the Wright Brothers to have built a ground cushion vehicle at the same time they flew the first aeroplane."

Not until the 1950s, however, did work on the ground-cushion concept finally come to the fore. The Avro Special Projects Group, under Frost's leadership, discovered the ground-cushion effect in 1953, while studying a flat-rising vertical-takeoff aircraft. Christopher Cockerell, a one-time staff member of Frost's in England, came upon the principles of ground cushion independently in 1954, as had Sir John Issac Thorneycroft nearly a century before, while making efforts to reduce the drag on ship hulls. Carl Weiland of Switzerland was working on the same principle by 1956.

Weapons System 606A in flight.
c. 1959 / Avro Aircraft Ltd.

HOVERCRAFT

Christopher Cockerell's experiments with coffee tins and a vacuum cleaner in the early 1950s led to the first manned hovercraft flight in 1959. The hovercraft is simply a vehicle that is wholly supported on a cushion of air supplied by a powered fan mounted on the craft. The cushion created by the fan is retained beneath the craft structure by a flexible extension to the craft structure, known as the skirt. The skirt is attached to the craft at the outer edge of the hull and at the lower edge of the planing surfaces. It is usually made from thin plastic-coated fabric and can be in the form of a tubular bag or separate, narrow segments. There are two types of hovercraft— those that use separate engines for lift and thrust and those that use one engine for both lift and thrust; the latter are known as integrated craft.

For an integrated craft, the engine and fan are usually mounted at the rear of the

Saunders Roe SRN5 hovercraft used on England-France cross-channel crossings.

1987 / Saunders Roe Company

hull, to balance out the driver sitting at the front. Around 25 percent of the air flow produced by the thrust fan is deflected by a horizontal splitter plate mounted in the air duct to provide the lift air. This lift air is ducted through the hull and fed underneath the craft to provide the cushion pressure and is retained by the skirt. Thrust and forward movement of the craft are achieved by the remaining 75 percent of the propulsion air, which is directed through the duct to the rear of the craft.

Hovercraft fitted with two engines usually have one at the front, which drives a fan to produce the lift air, and a much larger engine at the rear, to drive one or more propulsion fans. One major advantage of the twin-engine configuration is that it allows the craft to be on full cushion at all speeds, which provides much improved manoeuvrability. Both types of craft use rudders in the propulsion airflow for directional control. The pilot operates the rudder from the driving position by a deck-mounted joystick or a cycle-handlebar arrangement. The engines are controlled by lever-type throttles mounted on the joystick or handlebars.

The first hovercraft was the Saunders Roe SRN1 of 1959, which flew, but its limitations soon became apparent. It could not negotiate waves of more than 50 centimetres (20 in.) high or land obstacles more than 24 centimetres (10 in.) high. To combat these limitations, the flexible skirt was developed, and from then on hovercraft technology made rapid progress. In 1962 the Vickers VA3 provided a hover link across the River Dee from Rhyl to Merseyside; a forty-eight-passenger SRN2 operated across the Severn Estuary in 1963; and the first N5 operation across the Solent took place in 1964. Hovercraft have now become much larger and more efficient, and are in widespread use all over the world. Christopher Cockerell was knighted for his achievement in 1969.

Like all other interesting inventions, the hovercraft principle attracted many pioneer amateur builders. These pioneers eagerly experimented on a small scale with the new technology, eventually forming themselves into an organized group. In 1966, the Hoverclub of Great Britain came into being. A set of safety requirements was formulated for the design and construction of light hovercraft, and the responsibility for monitoring the development of light hovercraft was passed to the Hoverclub by the Civil Aviation Authority. Membership in the Hoverclub grew, branches were set up around the country and later, similar organizations appeared around the world.

Special events were organized where builders could put their one-place hovercraft through its paces and compare the latest technological developments. Car and motorcycle engines were used for the power units in those early craft and the centrifugal fans and propellers adapted for thrust units and hulls came in all shapes, sizes and materials. Most craft in those early days used two engines—one for lift and one for propulsion. Propellers were eventually discarded in favor of axial fans, and segmented skirts replaced bag skirts for racing hovercraft. For simplicity, lightness and efficiency, most of the smaller modern hovercraft are of an integrated design, powered by just one engine driving a single fan—just as in Cockerell's SRN1 back in 1959.

Hovercraft today are not only seen as private recreational craft but are also an integral part of countless commercial ferry systems worldwide and are key to many military armed forces tactical amphibious and waterborne operations. The Avrocar and the later Avroskimmer family could also have been successful hovercraft, if only....

A MODERN REAPPRAISAL OF THE AVROCAR

Douglas Garland, one of the Special Projects Group, described the technical difficulties of the Avrocar project recently:

Aerodynamic Problems Faced by the Avrocar Concept

Doug Garland, aerodynamicist-in-charge, Ames 40 x 80 wind tunnel tests

1. The Large Negative Static Margin

With a centre of gravity at or near the centre of the circular planform, for balance in hover, any circular wing at forward speed is fundamentally unstable longitudinally, that is, in pitch. For any kind of wing, the aerodynamic centre (where the lift forces act in forward speed) is well forward of the mid-chord point. It has to be aft of the c.g. for pitch stability, unless an aft tail surface or stabilizer is used. A tail was tried on the Avrocar during forward speed tests in the 40 x 80 foot wind tunnel at Ames but the large downwash close to the wing, where practically the tail had to be located, largely negated its effect on stability.

An unstable aircraft can be controlled provided it has an autostabilizing system of sufficient response rate and sufficient aerodynamic power.

To the best of my knowledge, the mechanical gyro-stabilized system with a rather weak jet flap pitch control on the Avrocar was not sufficient to do the job. The move from a Coanda type peripheral jet sheet to a focussing control ring was part of the effort to generate forward thrust from the focused jet under the disc. This was then bypassed at the rear when the jet flap type nozzle was used to improve lift at low speed and to provide a more powerful pitch control device.

Orenda static test rig for the Avro VZ-9-AV. The ground tests showed the first serious problems in thrust. c. 1958 / via Les Wilkinson

2. Wing Lift Efficiency

The circular wing is a low aspect ratio wing and suffers from a very low lift efficiency as do all low aspect ratio wings. The drag is very high for the amount of lift produced (the induced drag) and the angle of attack to generate a given lift is also high, which vectors the jet plume in the forward direction and makes it more difficult to get a favourable thrust-drag margin for acceleration.

The wing thickness was also fairly high, 18% I think, and the wing section had a blunt trailing edge, so that the profile drag was higher than a conventional wing.

3. Fan Effects at Forward Speed

The tip-turbine driven fan, designed and built at Orenda (I believe Prof. Jack Wade was involved with it) performed as expected on the test rig at Orenda, but as eventually installed in the Avrocar, it suffered from an effective exit area less than the design value. I think this was due to a redesign of the exit passage for the hot exhaust gases. Originally, these exited under the wing at or near the centre but for some reason were later ducted into the fan exhaust passages inside the wing, and the hot gases cut off the fan air passage. As a result, the fan was running off design and didn't reach its design thrust.

At forward speed in the wind tunnel, a large rolling moment was generated by asymmetric fan operation. The forward moving fan blades experienced a greater angle of attack than the retreating blades on the opposite side and generated more thrust. The internal ducts conveyed the higher fan pressure air to one side and the lower pressure air to the other side, resulting in a large rolling moment. Attempts were made to alleviate the problem by installing inlet guide vanes to turn the approaching air into the fan symmetrically. This helped a little but caused a large loss of fan thrust in hover.

Being a low pressure ratio fan (1.05 maybe) the duct and exit nozzle losses were significant, unlike typical jet engine ducts. The rectangular cross-section, multiple ducts, which formed the internal wing structure, were not the best from a pressure loss point of view.

4. Overall Assessment

The Avrocar would never have been an efficient cruising aircraft but if it had realized its potential as a high speed VTOL machine its unique capability might have outweighed its drawbacks.

5. Footnote

The Viper engines used in the engine development work for the rotary disc concepts were eventually declared surplus by the Canadian government and acquired by Don Whittley and the remnant of the Avrocar research engineers at de Havilland Canada in 1962 or a little later. They were put to very good use in the Augmentor Wing project when converted to "load compressors" driven by the exhaust of a J-85 engine. As such, they saw many years of wind tunnel tests at NASA Ames. The P470 project, which utilized multiple spanwise ducts, nozzles and wing slots, in a slender delta wing fighter, and was tested in the 6x9 foot tunnel at NAE, NRC, Ottawa, was a kind of precursor to the STOVL fighter designs developed by Don Whittley's group at de Havilland, in conjunction with various U.S. aircraft companies. These had longitudinal ducts, nozzles and slots. In 1987, when the 80x120 foot wind tunnel at Ames was unveiled to the public, the full-scale wind tunnel model sitting on the 40 foot high struts was a de Havilland lift-augmentor design installed in a highly modified General Dynamics F-16 airframe.

After John Frost and Des Earl left Avro in 1961, Don Whittley and Tom Higgins carried on the advanced projects group until what was left of Avro was taken into de Havilland Canada in August 1962, I think. The research group, under Don Whittley's leadership for many years, and finally under Joe Farbridge, ceased to exist in 1993, when the last research grants expired, Joe died suddenly of a heart attack, and some members were retired.

A more candid appraisal of the Avrocar was made by Peter G. Kappus, an aeronautical engineer who received the Paul E. Haueter Award in 1969. This award is given for significant contributions to the development of VTOL aircraft other than helicopters. In correspondence with Les Wilkinson, he reflected on the goals and accomplishments of the Avrocar project. "First, I must say that I was quite impressed by the thorough and competent engineering approach taken by Avro and Orenda in the development of this unorthodox vehicle," remarked Kappus. "As in all VTOL machines, stability and control in the hovermode turned out to be a challenge during the initial phase of flight testing. But after considerable modifications and improvements were accomplished, the

Avro team was obviously successful in giving the machine acceptable hover characteristics and reasonable control response in ground effect and at low speeds. Without detracting from these accomplishments, it must be said that similar results had been obtained during the same time period by other engineering teams using similar well established engineering principles.

"It is certainly remarkable that the tip turbine driven fan rotor, powered by three gas generators, held up mechanically throughout the extensive test program as well as it did. So, from a mechanical design aspect, the Avrocar, in spite of its unorthodox configuration and lift engine layout, was quite an accomplishment.

"It was, however, a dismal failure in its demonstrated performance capabilities. In contrast to its contractual objectives, it was never able to demonstrate hovering out of ground effect. Nor could it approach transition to wing supported free flight even at low airspeeds, not to mention the promised free flight capability at speeds over two hundred mph. All this in spite of a very substantial amount of installed power, conservatively estimated to be at least 2000 GHP (gas horsepower). This is probably due to the rather high internal duct losses inherent in the design concept and to the low aerodynamic efficiency of the disc shape. The vehicle could solely demonstrate the ability to operate as a controllable ground effect machine with very modest performance in speed and

"Spud" Potocki, Avro test pilot, flew the majority of the Avrocar test flights.   c. 1960 / via Les Wilkinson

payload. The same performance could have been achieved with a piston engine powered propeller driven ground effect machine at a fraction of the fuel consumption, engine cost and development effort required by the Avrocar.

"How was it possible that so much engineering effort and R&D finds were wasted in this manner? The Avrocar program is a classic example of what can happen if a hungry contractor with a good engineering team meets an Armed Forces organization with R&D funds to spend, looking for a 'technological breakthrough,' striving for a 'quantum jump' in performance capabilities through 'admittedly high risk development efforts.'

A very important catalyzer in this process is a smooth, highly persuasive inventor/promoter and an energetic military project officer with inadequate technical background but high enthusiasm for unorthodox novelties, in this case, undoubtedly intrigued by flying saucer lore."

Controls that were power boosted and utilized a computer sensor would have solved the Avrocar stability problems, and Avro was already at work on a reconfigured design that showed great promise, but it was too late.

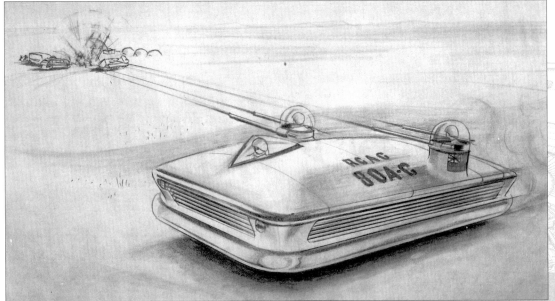

Left: Military Avrocruiser development of subsonic Avroskimmer family of vehicles. The artist's conception depicts a hovering "RCAC" (Royal Canadian Armoured Corps) version armed with recoiless weapons.

c. 1958 / via Les Wilkinson

Below: Avrocruiser. Combat vehicle development of subsonic Avroskimmer family of vehicles intended for use as a combat cargo, personnel, missile launching or weapons platform.

c. 1958 / via Les Wilkinson

AVRO CANADA'S OTHER SECRET PROJECTS

Ernie Happé, a design draftsman in the Special Projects Group, recalled that Frost had explored many areas in his saucer studies. He said that Frost "had wonderful ideas of developing it to become a passenger machine later on...carrying something like a thousand people as a hovercraft across the ocean. He also had ideas to take it up and bounce it off the layer of air around the Earth...he was full of bright ideas like that."

By 1958, Avro Canada VTOL projects had evolved into three distinct groups: the subsonic Avromobiles, made up of the Avrocar and its developments; the supersonic Avrodynes, the W/S 606A/PV 704 fighter projects; and an Avroskimmer family of vehicles that

Right: Avrowagon. Slightly larger vehicle development of subsonic Avroskimmer family of vehicles intended for private use.

c. 1958 / via Les Wilkinson

Below: Avrofliver. Vehicle development of subsonic Avroskimmer family of vehicles intended for private use over roads and rough terrain.

c. 1958 / via Les Wilkinson

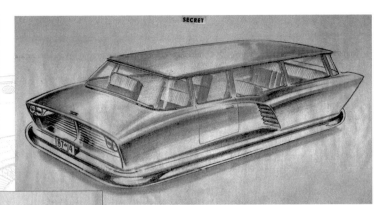

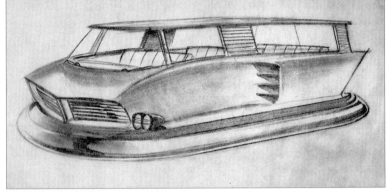

operated in a hovering or ground-cushion environment. One distinctive feature of this last group was the use of peripheral ducting rather than the flow-through ducted-fan approach of the Avrocar. This change allowed either piston engines or jet engines to power a rotor. The Avroskimmers were proposed as mainly tactical platforms and took on a variety of body shapes to suit the mission they flew. This family of vehicles was dependent on the Avrocar performing satisfactorily in tests prior to a go-ahead from the company. A final design concept also envisioned was the Avrodrone, a remote-controlled device that

also had GETOL ability, foreshadowing the unmanned reconnaissance aircraft of today.

A. V. Roe Canada proposed dozens of designs based on the Avromobile concept. They included commuter, emergency, surveillance, reconnaissance, anti-submarine and commercial transport versions. As Williams noted in 1976, "Frost eventually was talking about something the size of a jumbo jet to accommodate two hundred passengers. And why not?" However, these design studies did not proceed past conceptual stages. Another paper exercise was the Avro P450 Mobile Ground Effect Machine, more commonly known as the "Flying Ball." This appeared to be John Frost's last design for Avro Canada. Like most of his ideas, it was imaginative, daring and unconventional—a fitting testimony to the visions of John Frost.

A. V. Roe Canada was a shambles; nearly everyone had gone. Floyd went back to England, Chamberlin had gone to the NASA Apollo program (with about two dozen other Avro Canada engineers), Earl had been hired by Bell Aerospace (where he continued work on several ground-effect machines, including the "Bell bottomed Buffalo"—a de Havilland Canada DHC-5 Buffalo with an inflatable ground cushion skirt), Bryans went to the General Electric Company, and Potocki became a test pilot for North American Rockwell. As for Frost, he contemplated offers from abroad but delayed his decision for over a year. Over 10,000 others were still unemployed, and the vast plants of Avro Canada and the Orenda Division were virtually empty. Only the ongoing maintenance contracts of the CF-100 and its Orenda engine programs remained.

Avro Canada had many other projects left on the drawing boards. The Avro P470 was a more refined supersonic study based on a lift engine married to a delta-wing planform, which was envisioned as a tactical V/STOL reconnaissance/strike fighter for NATO service. Another project aimed at a NATO tactical strike-fighter role was the CF-100 STOVL Strike Aircraft, which utilized a CF-100 airframe and Bristol Orpheus lift-jets. The Avro 52 was designed as a small business jet (predating the Canadair [Bombardier] Challenger). Avro Canada had even proposed a licence-built Hunter Jet Provost jet-engined trainer as a competitor to the Canadair CL-41 design that would eventually become the Tutor. A. V. Roe Canada was looking for any program that would have a hope of success.

However, by 1961, efforts to sell the Orenda Iroqouis had failed, and attempts to diversify into new areas such as manufacture of pots and pans and boatbuilding were mainly uneconomic stop-gap measures. Like all of the final projects, they had promise, but the resolve and resources to develop them further were gone. The Avrocar had been the last aviation program of Avro Canada.

JOHN FROST'S STORY CONTINUED

As a result of his work in vertical-takeoff systems, John Frost was invited to become a fellow of the Canadian Aeronautics and Space Institute after he presented the W. Rupert Turnbull seventh lecture on May 25, 1961. The citation noted that Frost had discovered and patented the air-cushion effect that had been evident in his work on flying saucers and that U.S. Patent 3124323, "Aircraft Propulsion and Control," was one of a series of patents to become known as the "Frost patents."

But regardless of his stature in the scientific community, his days at A. V. Roe were numbered. With the end of the Avrocar project, he left the company early in 1962. At the time, he was resigned to his fate, but while on a *Front Page Challenge* televised interview, did characterize the loss of the project as a "tragedy to Canada...and a personal tragedy to me." As Ken Palfrey, a draftsman on the project, noted, "It was a sad story. He was a fine guy. A gentleman."

Shortly after Frost left Avro, the parent company, A. V. Roe Canada, which had been in the throes of disintegration for years, ceased to exist. On April 30, 1962, Sir Roy Dobson dissolved A. V. Roe Canada formally, and the remains of the once-proud company were transferred to the newly formed Hawker-Siddeley Canada Company. Avro Orenda Engines was reduced to a division of the new company, and the former Avro Canada plant at Malton was sold to de Havilland Aircraft (Canada) in 1962.

Like many of the former employees of A. V. Roe Canada, John Frost began a new career when he left the company. Following a lifetime interest in sailing, for a short period of time in 1963, Frost managed a boat business in Horseshoe Bay, Vancouver. In 1964, although he had become a naturalized Canadian citizen in the 1950s, he then left Canada permanently. Along with his wife, sons Christopher and Tony, and his daughter, Denise, he settled in Auckland, New Zealand. There, Frost again became part of the aviation industry, first joining the airworthiness section of the Civil Aviation Administration, where one of the projects that he headed was the certification of the Waitomo PL-11 Airtruck, the first commercial aircraft developed in New Zealand. He also designed the Murray Air, an agricultural biplane, for use in the Hawaiian Islands, and was responsible for the conversion of the Fletcher FU-24A to turbine power.

Later in 1965, frustrated by the pace of public-service bureaucracy, Frost became a technical-services engineer for Air New Zealand, serving in that position for thirteen years until his retirement in April 1978. His time at Air New Zealand was very fulfilling; he was responsible for all technical activities at the airline's engineering headquarters at Mangere, New Zealand. As reported in the *Daily News New Zealand* in April 1978, "Air New Zealand aircraft are showcases for the Frost ingenuity." The unique swiveling bassinets attached to the airliner's hat racks are his design, along with locks that hold down pallets in the cargo hold, air-conditioning systems for the cargo bay, rest seats for aircrew, toilet tap washers and gallery plugs. But his most impressive design was a gigantic $500,000 U.S. hydraulically operated tail-dock system, which acted like a dumbwaiter to raise 8 metres (26 ft.), to allow technicians to change the tail engine in aircraft such as the DC-10, which Air New Zealand was operating. The device was built at approximately half the cost of comparable equipment. Frost also designed a pit in the hangar floor to allow servicing of an aircraft undercarriage without raising the aircraft on jacks.

After Frost retired, his fertile imagination continued to explore many areas. Potential

John Frost at work in Air New Zealand.

c. 1979 / Air New Zealand

After Frost had satisfied himself with the results of his experiments with models, he then proceeded to build a full-size, 23.4-metre (80 ft.) wing-span aircraft in the workshop that he had enlarged for the purpose under his house. In early February 1979, two tests had been carried out—towing the machine behind a car—and after each test, some modifications to the wing incidence had been made. His collaborator, noted author Geoffrey Radcliffe, recalled recently, "We spent a lot of time together and finally completed the eighty-foot-span man-powered machine using the hangar at an (NZ) Air Force camp.... In days of your pre-computer times, there were inspired people like John who had an intuitive sense. Slide rules ruled the day. The third model...was very good at performing flat turns. It flew around the apple tree in John's garden and more than once, landed softly on John's daughter's Spaniel dog.... Our tests with a helicopter test pilot had John sitting in the open back of my car, holding some fishing line with a spring balance attached while we towed the EMME 1 off the ground."

After suffering a massive heart attack on October 9, 1979, John Carver Meadows

Frost died at the age of sixty-three. Around the world, obituaries marked his passing, although his true contributions to aeronautics were known only to a few insiders. After his death, the Royal New Zealand Air Force and the Aucklands branch of the Royal Aeronautical Society took over the Frost/EMME 1 project. The aircraft made a short flight but was damaged in a crash when the test pilot, F/Lt. Don Hamilton of the RNZAF, inadvertently crossed controls.

Tony Frost, his son, recalls, "After Dad's death, the University of Auckland took the project over, but they didn't seem to have the knack or know-how to get the project up and going again. The machine sits folded away in a box, in the Museum of Transport and Technology in Auckland, in a rather rusted, dilapidated condition." However, with its test flight, the last of John Frost's phenomenal aircraft designs had come to fruition. But as obituaries and commentaries after his death noted, his legacy will always be the dream of flying-saucer craft that nearly came true.

Avro Canada's secret projects showed the amazing technological virtuosity and visionary promise of this remarkable team of designers. Unlike many of these projects, the Avrocar was actually built and came close to success. Canada's "flying saucer" is today a historic footnote and only a memory to those who had known it, yet it was a fascinating glimpse of the future.

designs for yachts, underground industrial complexes and even a kit-based boat based on power from a wind-driven rotor were contemplated, before John Frost embarked on another exciting aviation project. With the assistance of university students in Auckland, he began the design of a human-powered aircraft—the Frost/EMME 1. "I have this idea...," Frost confided to a newspaper reporter with the *Daily News,* in 1978.

CHAPTER TEN

THE FUTURE TODAY

IN MANY WAYS, the Avrocar was a futuristic vision more within the realm of science fiction than science. It was the product of a period where anything was possible, and the near future was one of electric homes, space travel and flying cars. Scientists, scholars, and other visionaries made predictions in line with the rapid progress that was taking place in all areas of technology. And nowhere was the advance of science more amazing than in the field of transportation.

A hundred years before, it took three months to reach the other side of the planet, as described in the Jules Verne novel *Around the World in 80 Days*, set in 1872. By 1950, the same journey could take place in a jet airliner in less than a day, and scientists were already speculating on space travel that skimmed above the Earth. It was this idea of effortless travel that spawned some of the most extraordinary inventions.

FLYING CARS

The automobile had done more than any other device to shape the way ordinary individuals get around. However, scientists began to issue warnings in the late 1950s about the kind of world we would have if the automobile continued to dominate our lives.

In the secret design centres of major automobile companies, industry insiders knew that one day, alternate transportation vehicles had to be considered. In 1956, engineer Jim Powers at Ford built a scale model of a flying car—the Volante. Archival material from Ford records sketches of the original design and film of the model being built.

Today, the dream lives on. Dennis Bushnell, chief scientist for NASA at its Langley, Virginia, research headquarters has been quoted as saying he is "certain that the car has had its day, and that the skycar is the future."

MOLLER M400 SKYCAR

The most promising of the commuter aircraft currently being developed are those of Moller International, in Davis, California. For over thirty years, founder and Canadian expatriate, Paul Moller (former professor of mechanical engineering at the University of California), has been developing a series of flying saucers known as volantors (derived from volant, meaning having the ability to fly in a nimble, agile manner). His first one-passenger VTOL saucer, the XM-2, was completed in 1966. It demonstrated hovering ability and was followed in 1968 by the two-passenger XM-3, which used a single fan

The Moller M200X flight test. Moller International developed electronic stabilization systems and efficient ducted fans concurrently with its engine design. The company then constructed a manned, experimental two passenger volantor (M200X) to integrate these and other technologies and system components into a functioning saucer-shaped aircraft.

c. 1989 / Moller International

powered by eight engines. The first flight of the XM-3 achieved an altitude of 3 metres (10 ft.), and it could make a 360-degree turn. The next in the series, the XM-4, was powered by eight air-cooled rotary engines. A two-piece fiberglass airframe acted as a lifting body, while the thrust modules provided lift to hover and the impetus for forward flight. In test flights, Moller himself attained an altitude of over 10 metres (32.6 ft.) and sustained it for several minutes before setting back down again.

The Moller design formula is based on an inexpensive, easy-to-fly and extremely safe multi-engine platform. In 1992, Moller received the only generic patent ever issued in the U.S. on an entirely new aircraft type. This unique design is also the only aircraft presently considered by the FAA for certification under the new Powered Lift-Normal category. With more than 200 successful hovering and low-speed flights, years of research and over $60 million investment, the new two-man, eight-engined M200X volantor has proven the technical feasibility and reliability of the volantor design.

Subsequently, the company has built a radically different four-passenger volantor called the M400 Skycar, to meet the needs of the commuter of the future. This composite VTOL aircraft, like the M200X, uses Moller rotapower engines and company-developed electronic stabilization and fly-by-wire control systems. The Skycar combines the high-speed performance of 500 kilometres per hour

The Moller M400 Skycar with inventor, Paul Moller, in the cockpit. The Moller M400 is based on the knowledge gained from the M200X.

c. 1999 / Moller International

with VTOL capability and the practicality of a commuter vehicle in a single machine. Specifications call for cruise at up to 350 miles per hour, top speed of 390 miles per hour, a ceiling of 30,000 feet, a range of 900 miles and over 20 miles per gallon on standard gasoline.

The M400 Skycar features a Moller-patented system of variable-camber exit-duct vanes that direct thrust from seven-bladed, variable-speed fans mounted on each engine to produce lift for vertical takeoff and hovering. Three on-board computers adjust the stability for hover and the vanes in flight for lift or forward motion. Each of the four nacelles surrounding the fuselage contains two engines, with synchronized, counter-rotating fans that face each other to confine prop-tip

noise to the centre of each nacelle. Another Moller invention, the Supertrapp muffler, keeps noise down to less than 30 percent of that from a light aircraft at takeoff.

With rugged plastic construction, the Skycar is also designed for safe and simple use. Computer-enhanced flight controls are based on a lever, which is used to select altitude and rate of climb, and a control column for directional control. Only a few hours of training and computer simulation will prepare the pilot/operator for a first flight.

Normal operation would probably involve short commuter flights. Should engine failure occur during flight, the Skycar can glide or use an emergency ballistic parachute system.

Melvin D. Saunders wrote about the Moller projects in 1999, noting that "Moller says that all of the technical problems have been solved, and that product liability and production money are the only limiting factors left." The Moller 400 Skycar has attracted interest not only from future owners and investors, but also the military and scientific communities. The enticing possibility of creating an aerial commuter craft has led to discussions of the future of private transportation devices and has again rekindled interest in the military applications of a practical flying jeep that incorporates VTOL capabilities and high performance.

The Moller Aerobot UAV platform. Moller has designed and demonstrated several different configurations in both electric- and fuel- powered versions of the Aerobot under contract from military, federal , and state agencies.

c. 1989 / Moller International

AEROBOT

MODERN FLYING SAUCERS
Moller Aerobots
Although the Moller vehicles have incorporated more conventional aircraft shapes, the lure of the saucer continues. Since the mid-1980s, Moller International has also developed a series of small, unmanned aerial vehicles (UAVs) called Aerobots.

Aerobots have been developed into six different configurations, including a saucer or circular disc. They use the ducted fan and stabilization and control technology developed by Paul Moller to provide vertical takeoff and landing, hover, and transition flight ability.

Moller Aerobots are ideally suited for remote sensing, observation, inspection, and photography. They can also be capable of operating entirely autonomously as airborne robots, or semi-autonomously as remotely controlled aerial platforms. As simple to operate, stable, aerial platforms, the UAVs are able to operate from unimproved sites without special launch or recovery equipment, and are easily controlled by a single operator. Aerobots can hover at a fixed point or move horizontally at moderate speeds, and are very safe and quiet due to their advanced ducted-fan technology.

Sikorsky Cypher
In many respects, the robotic heir to the Avrocar, another UAV called the Cypher, was first flown in the summer of 1988. Sikorsky Aircraft has been testing this 1.83-metre-diameter (6 ft.), disc-shaped unmanned

Sikorsky Cypher UAV presently in test.

c. 2000 / Sikorsky Aviation

reconnaissance vehicle. It is clearly a flying platform in general concept, with a doughnut-shaped shroud that not only improves safety in handling the machine, but also helps increase lift. The Cypher, with maneouvrability that lets it lurk around terrain features, is powered by a four-stroke, 3.8-horsepower engine, and is based on coaxial-rotor technology developed by the company in the early 1970s.

The first proof-of-concept Cypher was 1.75 metres (5.74 ft.) in diameter and 55 centimetres (21.65 in.) tall, weighed 20 kilograms (44 lbs.), and was mounted on a truck for forward-flight tests. It led in turn to a second-generation Cypher that weighs 110 kilograms (242 lbs.) and is powered by a compact, 53-horsepower Wankel engine. Sikorsky has used the Cypher as a test platform for new technologies utilizing advanced soft-ware for highly autonomous operation. The design is highly manoeuvrable and capable of flying down city streets and other tight places. It is easily launched and recovered, and can be handled by two soldiers using a Hummer vehicle as a transport and control system. Sikorsky have no production contract for it at this time.

Williams International Wasp II

Piloted flying platforms are still being considered; new developments include a design that dates back before 1956, when conceptualized models were first being constructed (U.S. Patent 2,953,321—"The Flying Platform" by Robertson, Stuart III and Wagner). The U.S. Army paid over $2 million for Williams International to develop the first two test machines, in a quest for greater mobility of military personnel in the field. A more modern model, the Wasp II, has a midget turbofan engine that was designed and developed by Williams. The small engine produces thrust in the 272-kilogram (600 lb.) class and is completely enclosed in front of the operator.

The pilot/operator walks up to the free-standing vehicle, steps onto a small platform, takes the hand control, starts the engine and flies. The Wasp II is designed to take off vertically and fly for thirty minutes at speeds up to 97 kilometres per hour (60 m.p.h.). During flight, the vehicle is controlled by the pilot leaning in the desired direction, experiencing a natural sense of balance. The compact device has no wings or exposed rotors, allowing the operator to fly between and under trees, close to buildings and cliffs, and to reach areas that helicopters and other transport devices cannot reach. It can land on a 1.2-metre-square (4 ft.^{2}) area.

Flying Jeeps

Even the flying jeep is being revived. An Israeli company named Aero-Design & Development (AD&D) is also developing a flying-jeep platform named the Hummingbird that appears remarkably similar to the Hiller Pawnee designs. AD&D officials are not worried about the practicality of a one-person flying platform, since they are developing the Hummingbird as a recreational vehicle. They hope to reduce its weight to under 115 kilograms (254 pounds), to allow it to be sold in the U.S. as an ultralight aircraft. AD&D intends to sell the aircraft as a complete kit for $30,000 U.S.

The Hummingbird is built using modern technologies such as a composite airframe to reduce weight. It is powered by four single-cylinder piston engines, driving two contra-rotating propellers through a digitally controlled central gearbox. The four engines are a safety measure, as is an emergency parachute fitted to the vehicle. Noise reduction is a high priority. The Hummingbird's duct is 2.2 metres (7.2 ft.) wide, and expected endurance is about forty-five minutes, with a top speed of at least 45 kilometres per hour (25 knots).

Saratov Ekip

The Avrocar was a genuine flying saucer, and now the same principles are being used in the heart of the former Soviet Union. At the once top-secret Saratov Aerospace Factory in Russia, a craft called an Ekip has been built, which looks like a flying saucer. Its inventors believe that one day it will be a serious rival to conventional airliners, with a final version capable of carrying 2,500 passengers.

Ren TV in Russia reported that Saratov engineers had developed a small prototype craft in 1997, describing their invention as "an absolutely a new concept of flying." An air-cushion system would allow it almost vertical takeoff and landing. They claimed "the new aircraft is fundamentally different from all means of transportation known so far." The original concept for the saucer, named

Saratov Ekip flying saucer was constructed in the late 1990s but is now awaiting further financing.   c. 2000 / Ren TV

"Ecology and Progress," envisaged a craft that could move at 700 kilometres per hour (435 m.p.h.), could accommodate up to 1,000 people, and land anywhere, including mountainous terrain or water. The Saratov Ekip project has now been shelved for lack of funds, but the factory has stored the prototype in the hope that eventually development may proceed.

Doak Flying Discs

Edmund Doak was also contracted by the USAF to develop disc-shaped airfoil aircraft in the 1950s and 1960s. His last and most promising, the Doak-16, was cancelled by the USAF in the 1960s.

Had high-performance saucers like Weapon System 606A marked the end of large-scale military saucer research? William Blake, an aerospace engineer at the Air Force Research Laboratory, Wright-Patterson Air Force Base, has detailed information about a huge nuclear-powered saucer craft designed by Convair in the early 1960s under a Navy contract for a transoceanic transport. He came across a brief article dated June 1960, which shows a general arrangement drawing, and describes the vehicle as 122 metres (400 ft.) in diameter and capable of carrying an amazing 453,592-kilogram (million-pound) payload. Known as a ground-effect machine, or GEM, the concept relied on a "curtain-jet," like the Avrocar, for lift near the ground, but had no provision for flight at higher altitudes.

The Airship

Even lighter-than-air craft have investigated the use of a saucer shape in a number of unique projects. Inventor Brian Motts has been working on a craft that would combine futuristic technology with the travel experience of a bygone age. His saucer-shaped airship would be driven not by propellers, but by the mysteries of "ion propulsion," which date back from the "levitation experiments" of the 1950s. Russian designers have recently adopted a shape strikingly reminiscent of Lockheed's 1953 patent for a saucer craft to make their huge Thermoplane cargo blimps stable at low speeds and efficient at high speeds.

The Lightcraft

At the Rensselaer Polytechnic Institute Laboratory in New York State, fantasy is about to become fact. The lab is presently testing the revolutionary Lightcraft, incorporating advanced propulsion and drag-reduction concepts designed by aerospace engineer Prof. Leik Myrabo. The tiny, saucer-like craft uses an ultra-sophisticated propulsion system called magneto-hydrodynamics, which many UFOlogists believe has been around for years as the driving force behind alien spacecraft. The lightcraft has no propellant on board, will get its power from microwaves (lasers) directed towards it from satellites in space, and will be able to travel at twenty-five times the speed of sound.

If the entire concept seems like something out of a science-fiction story, that's because it started out that way. It was the cover of a sixty-five-year-old pulp-fiction magazine that first inspired Myrabo to think about ways of beaming power directly to spacecraft. He believes the Lightcraft will be the next wave of spacecraft design—a saucer that rises to orbit powered by a laser beam. The Lightcraft Technology Demonstrator (LTD) is at the testing stage today. Air Force Research Laboratory's Propulsion Directorate at Edwards Air Force Base, California, and the National Aeronautics and Space Administration's Marshall Space Flight Center at Huntsville, Alabama, are jointly developing the LTD concept for launching one-kilogram nanosatellites, and eventually microsatellites weighing up to one hundred kilograms, into low Earth orbit.

The Lightcraft propulsion concept works by focussing laser light to a ring focal point at the inner surface of a shroud. The focussed laser light forms an intense high-temperature plasma circle. This plasma literally explodes out the rear of the Lightcraft, creating a short pulse of very high thrust, at a rate of twenty-eight times per second. In between laser detonations, fresh air rushes into the cavity, where the laser is focussed to again be detonated.

There are Lightcraft vehicles that are currently being tested. They use only the atmospheric air available to them as they are launched to higher and higher altitudes. Rocket engineers would say that this Lightcraft vehicle has an infinite specific impulse.

The first phase of the LTD program began during the summer of 1996 and was completed in December 1998. The first experiments with a 20-centimetre (7.9 in.) Lightcraft weighing 2 kilograms (4.4 pounds) were conducted in July 1996 at the High Energy Laser System Test Facility, White Sands Missile Range, New Mexico. The second phase of the LTD program began in January 1999, and test results have shown that the Lightcraft has been successful in meeting its initial design objectives. John Mankins, a space-flight expert from NASA, believes that the Lightcraft has a lot of potential, and may become the saucer of the future.

THE AVROCAR STORY CONTINUES

Amazingly, the story of the Avrocar lives on, as countless UFOlogists have recounted the design of the Avro VTOL projects as part of the "UFO conspiracy." Trading on the story of the Avrocar were the news releases in late March and early April 1998 about Project Snowflake, which detailed an alleged top-secret flying-saucer program operating in the 1970s near Gilton, Alberta. Project Snowflake was rumoured to have been a $136-million initiative to develop a Canadian flying-saucer-style surveillance vehicle. Similar in

Artist's conception of the Lightcraft.

1999 / Rensselear Polytechnic Institute

appearance to the Avrocar flying disc, it was reputed to incorporate a revolutionary lifting and propulsion system. Poisson Aerospace, a Canadian aerospace company, was said to have conducted this top-secret program from 1971 to 1975. During this time, a working prototype of the craft was allegedly developed and flight tested at night, in and around their test site. Poisson executives decided to scrap Project Snowflake after stories began to circulate about local farmers seeing strange lights in the sky at night and the discovery of circular markings in the snow.

Project Snowflake was subsequently revealed as an April Fool's Internet stunt by the staff at Discovery Channel's EXN.ca website. Mixing the facts about Canada's research efforts in the late 1950s that resulted in the Avrocar project and major-league, tongue-in-cheek fiction had resulted in a surprising number of Internet visitors to their site being taken in by the hoax. Intended only to promote the re-launch of the award-winning science site, instead, the hoaxers found that with the inventive telling of the tale and release of "secret" data and photographs, they had convinced a sizeable majority of the population. In conducting the stunt, they learned that 63 percent of respondents believe that UFOs exist, 63 percent think that UFO technology exists on Earth and 74 percent of Canadians polled believe that governments are hiding UFO technology. Like Project Snowflake, Gilton, Alberta also did not exist, but most Internet surfers were

willing to pass on the information as fact, and for a year, information about Project Snowflake appeared on countless sites.

As recently as this year, publications have referred to the Avrocar as being a mock project that was intended to deceive the public as to the true intentions of the U.S. military in "black projects" linked to the Area 51 complex in Nevada. The speculation has included Canadian sources that postulate that the Avrocar was more successful than imagined, or was the portent of things to come.

These wide-eyed "imagineers" had been the bane of the Special Projects Group, as the members had had to deal constantly with media conjecture about the research they were undertaking in their VTOL studies. Both Ernest Ball and Des Earl, former members of the Avro Canada Special Projects Group, dealt with that issue in a 1993 CBC documentary *It Came from Malton*, saying, "We weren't trying to build a flying saucer—it was an aircraft project."

Recently, astronomer and educator Chris Rutkowski, in looking at the theories linking the Avrocar project to man-made saucers, said that he "couldn't buy it—there was not any real evidence cited by various authorities." Yet the debate continues still.

HANSSADYNE AEROSCIENCE HSDX LENTICULAR AERODYNE

One current research-and-development program has been directly based on the Avrocar and Weapons Systems 606A supersonic

circular-airfoil data, as well as related fan rotor data. Hanssadyne Aeroscience was formed by a group of aerospace engineers who began formal research to build a flying-saucer aircraft at the University of Texas at Arlington, over ten years ago. The Hanssadyne HSDX Lenticular Aerodyne is the brainchild of Douglas J. Hance, Jr., who has endeavoured to finance an ambitious saucer-craft project since the early 1990s. Hance claims it has an "advanced propulsion system and aerodynamic effects far superior to even the most advanced jet aircraft that have ever flown." And although scale models have been constructed that show the general dimensions and configuration of the proposed vehicle, test flying of a concept demonstrator model has not proceeded at present. However, a detailed report on the research effort and a complete illustrated history of earlier major circular-aircraft designs has been offered on the Internet by the company, to help finance future development.

Overleaf: Military Avrocar. Combat vehicle development of the Avrocar. The illustration shows a pair of Avrocars armed with recoiless weapons working as tank-busters in a "nap of the earth" attack. c. 1958 / via Les Wilkinson

CREDITS

THE AUTHOR

Bill Zuk is an aviation historian and writer who has a long-standing interest in aviation. Currently a teacher/librarian in St. Vital School Division, Winnipeg, he is also an active member of a number of associations involved in literature and aviation history. When the Straight Arrow production team began work in Winnipeg in 1997, he asked for and received permission to chronicle the making of the Arrow film. His work has also appeared in various publications, including *The Avro CF-100* by Larry Milberry.

"Writing for pleasure continues to be an area that I have enjoyed, one of my latest projects being the writing of a murder mystery play that was recently staged at a Victorian home in Winnipeg. I consider myself an amateur historian and my work continues to include nonfiction magazine articles for various publications on historical subjects. I have also written three childrens books— one on Terry Fox, a child's guide to a museum and a picture book on the Avro Arrow. These and future writing projects are being considered for later publication.

THE COLLABORATOR

Leslie (Les) Wilkinson was born in 1922 in Farnborough, England. He spent his youth peering over the fence at the airplanes famed Farnborough aerodrome, and it was not very surprising that when war came, he enlisted in the RAF as a pilot in 1941. Les was sent to Canada to train in the British Commonwealth Air Training Plan (BCATP) on multi-engine Airspeed Oxfords, receiving his wings in October 1943. But he remained here as a BCATP flight instructor and later test pilot in a Service Flying Training School in Alberta. In 1944, Les trained on the west coast on Convair B-24 Liberators before he travelled across Canada by rail to get married in Toronto to Marion MacKay. He then became a Liberator pilot in the China-Burma theatre, arriving in India in 1945 just as the atomic bombs fell.

After being demobilized in England, he came back to Canada in 1946 to begin a family and a new career in elevator maintenance at Beckett-Schindler Elevators in Toronto. Les, Marion, sons Peter and David, and daughter Patricia, lived in Weston, in the shadow of the great Avro Canada plant. Les loved aviation passionately and became a national director of the Canadian Aviation Historical Society, as well as their long-time secretary and librarian. He was also a member of the Burma Bomber Association, Aircrew Association, Legion Branch 266 Maple Leaf and was a Mason at the Islington Lodge.

His interest in Avro Canada, especially the story of the Avro Arrow, led to the co-authoring of *Arrow*, the preeminent book on the subject. Since 1971, Les had researched the history of the Avro Canada Special Projects Group, travelling to England and the United States on numerous occasions. Mainly using Freedom of Information Acts, he amassed nearly a thousand documents and related material culled from Canadian, British and American sources on John Frost and his work.

After suffering a heart attack at a dinner of the Burma Bomber Association, Les Wilkinson died on March 29, 1999. This book is dedicated to him and his efforts to tell the story of Canada's flying-saucer projects and the people who had dreamed that dream.

Overleaf: View of aircraft landing. Weapons System 606A.   c. 1959 / via Avro Aircraft Ltd.

THE STORY CONTINUES...

BRINGING CANADA'S SAUCER BACK HOME

Both Avrocars are still intact, and survive in U.S. museums. The first Avrocar, S/N 58-7055, the unmanned test rig and wind-tunnel test vehicle marked as AV-7055, was never flown. It was shipped to the NASA Ames Research Center Wind Tunnel at Moffatt Field, California, in 1960. After wind-tunnel testing, it remained for years in storage at the NASA facility, before being donated to the National Air and Space Museum. In 1966, Maj. Gen. C. Demler, commander of the Research and Technology Division, Air Force Systems Command at Bolling Air Force Base, D.C., wrote to S. Paul Johnston, then director of the National Air Museum (now the National Air and Space Museum) of the Smithsonian Institute in Washington, D.C., to offer this example of the Avrocar for preservation. Today AV-7055 is stored in Building 22 of the NASM Paul E. Garber Facility, in Silver Hills, Maryland, along with other notable experimental vehicles such as the Convair XFY-1 Pogo and the Gotha Go 229 (Horten IX) flying wing.

The Garber storage and restoration facility is open to the public, and although the Avrocar is on display, at present its access is limited, as the aircraft sits under the wing of another aircraft, a Northrop P-61 Black Widow. The disc is corroded and covered in layers of dust. The main structure is there but canopies, cockpit instrumentation and access panels are missing. Only a placard indicating its name and brief note about its history are provided. The "flying saucer," as it is referred to at the NASM, is mainly neglected and relegated to being an object of historical curiosity or oddity. Jack Walker, tour guide, patiently explains to visitors, "I have no idea why anyone would want to see that thing—it never really worked, you know." According to curator Russell Lee, the NASM Avrocar is slated for restoration prior to its anticipated display at the new Dulles facility being planned for 2003 and beyond.

The second Avrocar, S/N 59-4975, representing the sole flying example of the type, was stored from 1966 at the U.S. Army Aviation Materials Laboratories at the U.S. Army Transportation Museum at Fort Eustis, Virginia. For a short period of time, this Avrocar was on loan to the Canadian government, as the second prototype was displayed in 1969 at the Man and His World Exhibit in Montreal, a continuing exhibition following the successful Expo '67 World's Fair in Montreal. At the end of the display, the Avrocar was again returned to Fort Eustis for storage. The U.S. Army Transportation Museum at Fort Eustis received the Avrocar in 1979. Billed as housing the world's only captive flying saucer, the museum features other important exhibits, including the first helicopter to land at the South Pole, the Flying Crane (the Army's largest helicopter), and the de Havilland Canada Caribou, famed aircraft of the Golden Knights Army Parachute Team. The museum also contains other unusual artifacts related to the VTOL story, such as the Air Car Gem 2X, the de Lackner Aerocycle, the Piasecki 59H VZ-8P1 Airgeep flying jeep prototype, and a Bell rocket belt.

The second Avrocar is more prominently on display on pylons at the U.S. Army Transportation Museum at Fort Eustis, Virginia, as the central focus of the entranceway of the museum. However, after years of being out in the elements, the Avrocar is in decidedly poor shape and requires a great deal of maintenance due to its outdoor location.

It's time to bring Canada's flying saucer home! With the cancellation of the Avro

Canada CF-105 Arrow program and the destruction of aircraft, films, photographs and other records of the company leading to the final collapse of A. V. Roe Canada, Canadians lost a great part of our aviation industry and heritage. We have a sense that a wrong can still be made right.

You have the opportunity to petition the Minister of Canadian Heritage to intercede with the United States government in bringing back a part of our nation's aviation history from the National Air and Space Museum in Washington, D.C., or the U.S. Army Transportation Museum in Fort Eustis, Virginia.

Today in Toronto, the work of hundreds of volunteers, including the late Les Wilkinson, has resulted in the formation of the Toronto Aerospace Museum at the former Canadian Forces Base, Downsview. This museum is dedicated to preserving and displaying the aerospace heritage of Toronto, which includes the aircraft of the Curtiss, de Havilland Canada and Avro Canada companies that were once part of the city's aviation industry. Other Canadian museums that have expressed interest in the repatriation of one of the Avrocars include the National Aviation Museum in Ottawa, the Western Canada Aviation Museum in Winnipeg and the Canadian Warplane Heritage Museum, all of which presently display various Avro Canada artifacts.

The time to act is now. The agencies concerned, both in Canada and the United States, have shown interest in an Avrocar restoration and repatriation program. What a fitting tribute to bring back home to Canada a monument to the men and women of A. V. Roe Canada, whose final project was an aircraft of the future—our own "flying saucer." We have a chance to place it on display in its former home—for all to see and wonder about what was once a dream that almost came to be.

Direct your letter to the Minister of Canadian Heritage, House of Commons, Ottawa, Ontario, Canada K1A 0A6.

And what of John Carver Meadows Frost, the virtually unknown and unheralded creator of the Avro Canada Flying Saucer Projects? There is also an opportunity to recognize his contributions to Canada's aviation heritage through a nomination to Canada's Aviation Hall of Fame at the Reynolds-Alberta Museum, Wetaskawin, Alberta. The Aviation Hall of Fame originated in Calgary in 1973 and at its present-day location recognizes over 150 men and women who have made a historic or meaningful impact on our aviation heritage. Each year, the nomination committee calls for and accepts nominations from the public for new inductees. Their bylaws state that Canada's Aviation Hall of Fame "is open to those persons whose unselfish contributions to aviation shall have been of major benefit to Canada, and which contributions have stood the test of time." In 2001, the name of John Carver Meadows Frost will be submitted to mark his legacy in the story of A. V. Roe Canada as chief project designer of the Avro CF-100 Canuck and as chief designer of the Special Projects Group responsible for Avro Canada's VTOL programs.

A 1959 Christmas Card passed out at the Special Projects Group Christmas Party bore the following verse and image:

Merry Xmas
O Discobilo Novus,
And newer discus yet—
But not by dint of your strong arm,
But with reaction jet
This disc so very soon will fly—
A dream at last come true,
A dream of saucers in the sky—
And those designed by you.
At Christmas-time we send our wish
For many new ideas
In nineteen-fifty-nine, and then
Throughout the coming years.

The whimsical cartoon not only was a good likeness of "Jack" Frost, but also faithfully captured his trademark cowlick. The poem revealed the aspirations and dreams of this remarkable group of approximately one hundred engineers and technicians, and the esteem they held for their leader and friend.

BIBLIOGRAPHY

INTERVIEWS

Barker, Ed, Manitoba Provincial Director, MUFON (Mutual UFO Network). An introduction to the UFO Phenomenon. Lecture, Creative Retirement Seminar Series. Winnipeg: December 20, 1999.

Blake, William, engineer, Air Force Research Laboratory, Wright-Patterson Air Force Base. Telephone interview, January 24, 2000.

Caroline, Ken, Avro (U.K.) engineer. Written correspondence to Les Wilkinson, 1991 and 1992.

Campagna, Palmiro, author. Telephone interview, August 3, 1997.

Carpenter, Joel, author. Written correspondence, January 25, 2000.

Conway, John, engineer, Special Projects Group. Taped interview by Les Wilkinson, May 4, 1984.

Coyle, Bill, engineer, Special Projects Group. Telephone interview, August 2, 1997.

Dares, Alan C. author. Telephone interview, August 3, 1997.

Earl, T. Desmond, engineer, Special Projects Group. Taped interview by Les Wilkinson, August 2, 1983.

Elliot, George, president, Western Canada Aviation Museum. Personal interview, July 30, 1997.

Douglas Garland, engineer, Special Projects Group. Telephone interview, January 16, 2000. Internet correspondence, February 25, 2000.

Floyd, Jim, engineer, Avro Canada. Personal interview, Toronto: March 21, 1998.

Frost, Tony, John Frost's son. Telephone interview, March 17, 1999, and January 23, 2000.

Gilbertson, Fred, draftsman and engineer. Avro Canada, February 21, 2000.

Hance, Douglas J. Jr., president of Hanssadyne Aeroscience. Email correspondence, July 1999 and February 2000.

Hyslip, Doug, president, A. V. Roe Canada Heritage Museum. Interview by phone, September 16, 1999, written correspondence, November 16, 2000.

Johnson, Bob, technician, Avro Canada, and Ernest Nemeth, engineer, Special Projects Group. Recorded meeting: Canada's Flying Saucer, The Avro Canada Avrocar. Audio recording at the Toronto Chapter by Les Wilkinson, Canadian Aviation Historical Society, September 5, 1972.

Kappus, Peter G., NASA aeronautic engineer. Written correspondence to Les Wilkinson, January 11, 1984, and telephone interview, February 21, 2000.

Koerner, Steve, author. Telephone interview, September 30, 1997.

Lamar, Bill, engineer, Weapons Systems 606A. Telephone interview by Les Wilkinson, December 15, 1992.

Lindenbaum, Bernard, engineer, Weapons Systems 606A. Telephone interview, January 24, 2000.

McHaffie, Natalie, curator, Toronto Aerospace Museum. Personal interview, July 4, 1999.

McCrane, Frank, curator, U.S. Army Transportation Museum. Telephone interview, July 31, 1997, and February 2, 2000.

Mairsperger, Walter P., Lt-Col. USAF (ret.), Weapons Systems 606A. Taped interview by Les Wilkinson, March 10, 1984.

Milberry, Larry, author. Toronto. Telephone interview, August 1, 1997. various interviews, 1998, 1999.

Moller, Paul, president, Moller International. Telephone interview, February 7, 2000.

Muchnick, Howard, president, Canadian Warplane Heritage Museum. Telephone interview, February 9, 2000.

Murray, Colonel. Daniel C., project manager, Avrocar and Weapon Systems 606A. Telephone interview by Les Wilkinson, December 15, 1992.

Page, Ron D., author. Internet correspondence, January 24, 2000.

Payne, Stephen, curator, National Aviation Museum of Canada. Telephone interview. February 2, 2000.

Procter, Bill, engineer, Special Projects Group. Taped interview by Les Wilkinson, August 5, 1983.

Radcliffe, Geoffrey, author and pilot. Email correspondence, April 22–23, 2000.

Rogers, Don, chief test pilot, Avro Canada (ret.). Personal interview, Toronto, March 21, 1998.

Rutkowski, Chris, author. Reading and signing of "Abductions and Aliens: What's Really Going On?" McNally Robinson Booksellers. Winnipeg, January 17, 2000.

Stewart, Greig, author. Telephone interview, August 2, 1997.

Takeuchi, Ray, engineer, Special Projects Group. Telephone interview by Les Wilkinson, October 3, 1984.

Turner, Bill, engineer, Avro Canada. Telephone interview, August 1, 1997, and February 1, 2000.

Ward, Terry, head of acquisitions, Toronto Aerospace Museum. Telephone interview, July 8, 1999.

Waterton, W. A., test pilot, CF-100. Telephone interview. July 10, 1997.

Wheelband, Al, engineer, Special Projects Group. Taped interview by Les Wilkinson, July 1, 1983.

Wilkinson, Les, author. Telephone interview, July 8, 11, 1997, and personal interview, July 21, 1997, in Toronto.

Wright, Carolyn D., librarian, U.S. Army Transportation Museum. Telephone interview, September 16, 1997.

Wright, George, author. Telephone interview, August 13, 1997.

Zuuring, Peter, author. Personal interview, July 30, 1999, Winnipeg.

Zurakowski, Janusz, test pilot CF-100, CF-105 Arrow. Personal interview, May 30, 1997, Winnipeg.

BOOKS

Boyne, Walter J. *The Aircraft Treasures of Silver Hill*. New York: Rawson Associates, 1982.

Braybrook, Ray. *V/STOL: The Key to Survival*. London: Osprey, 1989.

Bryan, C. D. B. *The National Air and Space Museum*. New York: Harry N. Abrams Publishers, 1979.

Calvert, Denis J. *Harrier*. London: Ian Allen Limited, 1990.

Campagna, Palmiro. *Storms of Controversy*. Toronto: Stoddart, 1992.

―――. *The UFO Files: The Canadian Connection Exposed*. Toronto: Stoddart, 1997.

Chant, Christopher. *Fantastic Aircraft*. New York: Roydon Publishing, 1984.

Cramp, Leonard G. *Space, Gravity and the Flying Saucer*. New York: British Book Centre, 1955.

Dow, James. *The Arrow*. Toronto: James Lorrimer and Co., 1979.

Eggleston, Wilfrid. *Canada at Work*. Montreal: Canada at Work Publishers, 1953.

Floyd, Jim. *The Avro Canada C102 Jetliner*. Erin, Ontario: Boston Mills Press, 1986.

Gurney, Joseph. *Historical Overview of the Avro Aircraft Limited (Canada) Saucer Projects*. Unpublished manuscript, 1985.

Haber, Barbara Angle. *The National Air and Space Museum*. London: Bison Books, 1995.

Halion, Richard P. *Designers and Test Pilots*. Alexandria, Virginia: Time-Life Books, 1983.

Hunt, Leslie. *Veteran and Vintage Aircraft*. New York: Taplinger, 1970.

Jerram, Michael E. *Incredible Flying Machines*. London: Exeter Books, 1980.

Jackson, A. J. *Avro Aircraft since 1908*. London: Putnam, 1957.

McPeake, Wendy, ed. *The National Aviation Museum: A Flypast*. Ottawa: National Aviation Museum, 1991.

Milberry, Larry. *The Avro CF-100*. Toronto: CANAV Books, 1981.

―――. *Sixty Years: RCAF and CF Air Command 1924–1984*. Toronto: CANAV Books, 1984.

Oswald, Mary. *They Led the Way: Members of Canada's Aviation Hall of Fame*. Wetaskawin, Alberta: Canada's Aviation Hall of Fame, 1999.

Pace, Steve. *X-Fighters: USAF Experimental and Prototype Fighters XP-59 to YF-23*. Osceola, Wisconsin: Motorobooks International, 1991.

Page, Ron. *Canuck: CF100 All Weather Fighter*. Erin, Ontario: Boston Mills Press, 1981.

Peden, Murray. *Fall of An Arrow*. Toronto: Stoddart, 1978.

Robinson, Robert R. *Scrap Arrow*. Don Mills, Ontario: PaperJacks, 1975.

Rogers, Mike. *VTOL: Military Research Aircraft*. New York: Orion Books, 1989.

Rose, Arnold. *The Avrocar Story*. Unpublished manuscript, 1988.

Shainblum, Mark and John Dupuis, ed. *Arrow Dreams: An Anthology of Alternate Canadas*. Winnipeg: Nuage Editions, 1997.

Shaw, E. K. *There Never Was An Arrow*. Brampton, Ontario: Steel Rail, 1981.

Stewart, Greig. *Shutting Down the National Dream*. Scarborough, Ontario: McGraw-Hill Ryerson, 1988, 1997 (2nd ed.).

Vesco, Renato. *Intercept UFO*. New York: Zebra Publications, 1974.

Waterton, W. A. *The Quick and the Dead*. London: Frederick Mueller, 1958.

Wilkinson, Les, Ron Page, Richard Organ, and Don Watson. *Arrow*. Erin, Ontario: Boston Mills Press, 1980, 1993 (2nd ed.).

Wooldridge, E. T. *Winged Wonders*. Washington: National Air and Space Museum, 1983.

Wyatt, Daniel. *The Last Flight of the Arrow*. Toronto: Ballantine Books, 1990.

Yeager, Chuck, Bob Cardenas, Bob Hoover, Jack Russell, and James Young. *The Quest for Mach One: A First-person Account of Breaking the Sound Barrier*. New York: Penquin Books, 1997.

Zuuring, Peter. *The Arrow Scrapbook, a Dream and a Nation*. Arrow Alliance Press, 1999.

TECHNICAL PAPERS

Abbreviated Development Plan, AVRO Vertical Takeoff Aircraft, Weapon System 606A. Malton: Avro Aircraft Limited, 1960.

Avrocar Continuation Program. Data Report for 1/20 Scale Avrocar Model, 500/AERO TEST/410. Malton: Avro Aircraft Limited, April 20, 1962.

Avrocar Continuation Test Program, Avrocar 1. Malton: Avro Aircraft Limited, 1961.

Avrocar Continuation Test Program of an Avrocar in the 40 X 80 Foot Wind Tunnel at NASA Ames Research Center 500/AERO TEST/405, Issue 2. Malton: Avro Aircraft Limited, December 1960.

Avrocar Continuation Test Program Instrumentation Specification for Ames Tunnel Tests 1st Avrocar Vehicle 500/AERO TEST/415. Malton: Avro Aircraft Limited, December 1960.

Chuprun, John Jr. *Trip Report*. Air Research and Development Command, Directorate of Systems Management, USAF, Wright-Patterson Air Force Base: January 4, 1960.

Deckert, W. H. and W. J. Hodgson. *Avrocar Flight Evaluation*. Air Force Flight Test Center, Edwards Air Force Base, United States Air Force: 1962.

Drinkwater, Fred, III. *Memorandum to Captain Daniel C. Murray, WS 606 Project Manager*. Wright-Patterson Air Force Base, March 22, 1960.

Earl, T. D. Brochure, *Avro Aircraft V.T.O.L. Aerial Jeep (Secret)*. Malton: Avro Aircraft Limited, October 30, 1957.

Earl, T. D. *Ground Effect Machines*. Malton: Avro Aircraft Limited, May 1961.

Engineering and Experimental Program for the Design and Development of Radial Thrust Jet Aircraft. Malton: Avro Aircraft Limited, 1956.

Frost, J. C. M. *United States Patent Office Patent 3,124,323 "Aircraft Propulsion and Control."* March 10, 1964.

Frost, J. C. M. and T. D. Earl. *Flow Phenomena of the Focused Annular Jet*. Malton: Avro Aircraft Limited, October 21. 1959.

Frost, J. C. M. and H. C. Moody. *Program Planning Report, AVRO VTOL Project PV 704*. Malton: Avro Aircraft Limited, July 1956.

Garland, D. B. *Avrocar Continuation Test Program Instrumentation Specification for Ames Tunnel Tests. 1st Avrocar Vehicle*. Malton: Avro Aircraft Limited, 1961.

———. *Studies of Ground Effect on an Inwardly Inclined Annular Jet*. Institute of Aerophysics, University of Toronto, August 1960.

Greif, R. K., M. W. Kelly, and W. H. Tolhurst Jr. *Wind Tunnel Tests of a Circular Wing with an Annular Nozzle in Proximity to the Ground*. Malton: Avro Aircraft Limited, 1961.

Greif, R. K., and William H. Tolhurst Jr. *Large-Scale Wind Tunnel Tests of a Circular Plan-Form Aircraft with a Peripheral Jet for Lift, Thrust and Control*. Malton: Avro Aircraft Limited, 1961.

Hall, Lt. Col. James N., and Capt. Daniel C. Murray. *Trip Report 59RZ-17786*. September 1, 1959.

Mertaugh, 1/Lt. Lawrence J. Jr. *Trip Report*. Air Research and Development Command, Directorate of Systems Management, USAF, Wright-Patterson Air Force Base: November 1, 1959.

Mordell, D. L. *Project Y: Preliminary Report on Aerodynamic Design and Performance, and Report on Acceleration and Starting Performance*. September 29 and November 1, 1952.

Murray, Captain Daniel C. *The Avro VZ-9 Experimental Aircraft: Lessons Learned*. Paper AIAA 90-3237 at the AIAA/AHS/ASEE Aircraft Design, Systems and Operations Conference. Dayton, Ohio: September 17–19, 1991.

———. *Trip Report 6ORDZ-3235*. Air Research and Development Command, Directorate of Systems Management, USAF, Wright-Patterson Air Force Base: February 17, 1960.

Program Planning Report Avrocar 1 United States Army Designation VZ-9AV Malton: Avro Aircraft Limited, May 1, 1958.

Progress Report #3 500/PROJ/6. Malton: Avro Aircraft Limited, November 1960.

Proposal for a Research and Development Program to Demonstrate Powered Lift System Potential. Malton: Avro Aircraft Limited, 1961.

Proposal for Further Development of the Avrocar, 500/PROP/13. Malton: Avro Aircraft Limited, June 1961.

Scientific Advisory Board to the Chief of Staff USAF, Scientific Advisory Board Report on AvroProject Y2. Department of the Air Force, December 1954.

Scott, W. J. *Asymmetry of Annular Jet Flow in Ground Proximity, Part I: 60 deg. Inwardly Inclined Annular Jet Hovering at Zero Angle of Attack.* Malton: Avro Aircraft Limited, 1961.

Sliding Ring Focuses Flying Saucer Thrust. Malton: Avro Aircraft Limited, 1960.

Smith, R. E. *Studies of Ground Effect on a 60 deg. Inwardly Inclined Annular Jet, Part II: Base Plate Thrust Augmentation and Pressure Distribution Effects of Aspect Ratio, Pressure Ratio and Height Above Ground, Jet Stability.* Malton: Avro Aircraft Limited, 1961.

Stephens, W. R. *Asymmetry of Annular Jet Flow in Ground Proximity, Part II: A Static 60 deg. Inwardly Inclined Annular Jet Hovering at an Angle of Attack.* Malton: Avro Aircraft Limited, 1960.

———. *Review of Commercial VTOL Aircraft Development Possibilities.* Malton: Avro Aircraft Limited, 1960.

———. *A Review of Promising Future Avro Projects.* Malton: Avro Aircraft Limited, 1960.

———. *U.S. Army Requirement for a New Family of Air Vehicles.* Malton: Avro Aircraft Limited, 1959.

Technical Report No. TR-AC-47, Joint ATIC-WADC, Report on Project Silver Bug, Project No. 9961. Published by Air Technical Intelligence Center, Wright-Patterson Air Force Base, Ohio: February 15, 1955.

Thomas R. D. *Background of the Avrocar Program.* Malton: Avro Aircraft Limited, 1959.

Woodman, Jack. *Flying The Avro Arrow.* Canadian Aeronautics and Space Institute Symposium, Winnipeg: May 16, 1978.

Zipkin, M. Z., R. J. Rossbach, and H. Brown. *Convertible Turbojet Engines for VTOL Aircraft.* Malton: Avro Aircraft Limited, 1959.

MAGAZINE ARTICLES

"Aero Patents." *Air Progress*, April–May 1964.

"Avro Aircraft Saucer." *Aircraft*, Dec. 1955.

"Avro Arrow Design." *The Aeroplane*, Oct. 10, 1958.

"Avro Canada's Omega." *The Aeroplane*, May 1, 1953: 569.

"Avro Tests Ground Cushion Vehicle." *Aviation Week*, Nov. 9, 1959: 104.

"The Avrocar Revealed." *Aircraft*, Oct. 1960: 39.

"Avro's Saucer." *Canadian Aviation*, Sept. 1960: 54.

Ball, Ernest. "The (Almost) Flying Saucer." *Air Enthusiast International*, Vol. 6 No. 6, June 1974: 300–301.

Barker, Gray. "A Report on Flying Saucers." *The Saucerian Review*, Jan. 1956.

Berliner, Don. "The UFO from the Designer's Viewpoint." *Air Progress*, Oct. 1967.

Blake, William B. "The Avro VZ-9 'Flying Saucer.'" *Skeptical Inquirer*, Spring 1992: 297–291.

Boniface, Patrick. "Tit-wing Testing." *Aeroplane*, March 2000: 72–78.

Brown, Eric, "An Ill-fated 'Swallow.'" *Air Enthusiast*, 10: 1–7.

Caidin, Martin. "The Coanda Story." *Flying*, May 1956: 32–33, 50, 54, 56–58.

"Canada Builds a Flying Saucer." *Fate*, Oct. 1953: 14–17.

"Canadian 'Saucer' may be Delta Fighter." *Air Pictorial*, May 1953.

"Chance Vought XF5U-1 Skimmer." *Air Progress*, April–May, 1964.

Dane, Abe. "Flying Saucers: The Real Story." *Popular Mechanics*, Jan. 1995: 50–53.

Dares, Alan C. "The VZ-9V Avrocar 'Flying Saucer.'" *C.A.H.S. Journal*, Spring 1993: 26–28.

"Disc-Shaped Avrocar." *Air Pictorial*, Oct. 1960: 344.

"Disc-Shaped Vehicles are Studied for Potential as Orbital Aircraft." *Aviation Week*, Aug. 15, 1960.

Douglass, Robert G. "Flying Saucers from Canada." *American Heritage of Invention and Technology*, Winter 1996: 58–63.

Earl, T. Desmond. "Obituary: John Carver Meadows Frost." *Canadian Aeronautics and Space Journal*, Vol. 26, No. 2, Second Quarter, 1980.

"The First Real Saucer?" *Royal Air Force Flying Review*, 1961: 22.

Frost, J. C. M. "Avrocar Chapter: Canadian Contribution to the Ground Cushion Story." *Aircraft*, July 1961: 8–10, 12.

———. "Canadian Contribution to the Ground Cushion Story." *Canadian Aeronautical Journal*, October 1961: 286–302.

———. "Proving Out a Flying Saucer." *Canadian Aviation*, July 1961: 14–18.

Gale, John. "Farnborough Newcomer." *Jet Age*, Autumn 1955.

Gerhardt, George. "Soldiers in the Sky." *Air Progress*, Spring 1962.

Green, William. "VTOL 1962." *Royal Air Force Flying Review*, Vol. XVII, No. 6: 15–17, 40, 46, 48.

"Ground Effect Machines." *Air Progress*, Spring 1960: 32–34.

Hansard. House of Commons, Feb. 20, 1959.

"Is this the Real Flying Saucer?" *Look*, Vol. 19, June 14, 1955.

Jenkins, Peter. "Hall's Selection Process Demystified." *The Flyer, Canada's Aviation Hall of Fame at the Reynolds-Alberta Museum*, Wetaskawin, Alberta, 1999: 1–2.

Keene, Tony. "Canada's Forgotten Arrow." *Air Classics* , Vol. 25, No.1, Jan. 1989: 26–31, 80– 81.

Lake, Jon. "BAE Systems Sea Harrier." *World Air Power Journal*, Vol. 41, Summer 2000: 60–102.

Ley, Willy. "How the Flying Saucer Works." *Mechanix Illustrated*, March 1956: 78–81.

Lloyd, Paul. "The Wildest of Dreams." *Scale Aircraft Modelling*, Vol. 21, No. 11, Jan. 2000.

Lyzun, Jim. "From Warhorse to Workhorse." *Air Enthusiast*, March/April 2000: 16–26

Macleod, Neil. 'Do 'Flying Saucers' Have Any Meaning?" *Eilean an Fhraoich Annual*, Dec. 1947.

"Man-made Flying Saucer." *Royal Air Force Flying Review*, April 1953: 11–12.

Mellberg, Bill. "Too Good to be True." *Air Enthusiast*, No. 54, 1994.

"Muscles in the Sky." *Mechanix Illustrated*, Sept. 1957.

"Now See This." *Mechanix Illustrated*, June 1959.

Pace, Steve. "Supersonic Cavaliers." *Airpower*, November 1986: 24–43, 50–53.

Peden, Murray. "Fall of the Arrow Pt. 1." *Wings*, Vol. 9, No.1, Feb. 1979: 10–24, 59, 62–63, "Pt. 2" *Airpower*, Vol. 9, No. 2, March 1979: 30–43, "Pt. 3" *Wings*, Vol. 9, No. 2, April 1979: 24–29, 55.

Pelletier, Alain J. "Towards the Ideal Aircraft, Part Two." *Air Enthusiast*, Sept.–Oct. 1996: 8–20.

"Princeton's Gems." *Air Progress*, Spring 1961: 54–55.

"Project Y." *Aircraft*, March 1956.

Rankin-Lowe, Jeff. "Avro Canada CF-100 Variants." *Wings of Fame*, Vol. 18: 102–132

Rudy, John Forney. "The Flying Pancake." *Air Trails and Science Frontiers*, June 1947: 42–43, 68.

Solomon, Stan. "When a Pancake Flew." *Aviation History*, Sept. 1997: 46–52.

Stine, G. Harry. "The Amazing Mr. Coanda." *Air Progress*, Aug./Sept. 1965: 6–12.

"Straight up from Malton." *Aircraft*, March 1961: 31, 56.

Stover, Dawn. "50 Years after Roswell." *Popular Science*, June 1997: 82–88.

"Untossed Pancake: the Story of the Ill-fated XF5U-1." *Air Enthusiast*, June 1973: 287–293.

Young, Scott. "The Way Up: An Account of the 10-year History of A.V. Roe Canada Limited." *Jet Age*, Winter: 5–12, 16–25.

Webb, Derek Collier. "Tested and Failed." *Aeroplane*, Jan. 1998: 12–15.

Wilson, Tom. "Canada's Jet Warrior Pt. 1." *Air Classics*, Vol. 16, No.3, March 1980: 24–33, "Pt.2" Vol. 16, No.4, April 1980: 70–77, 82.

Zuk, Bill, "The Avro Arrow on Centre Stage." *Airforce*, Winter 1997: 4–11.

NEWSPAPER ARTICLES

"A. V. Roe Pins Hopes on 'Flying Saucer.'" *Financial Post*, March 21, 1960.

"Avro Pins Hopes on "Saucer.'" *Financial Post*, Nov. 7, 1959.

Barkway, Michael. "Ottawa May Give Cash Aid to Avro's 'Flying Saucer.'" *Financial Post*, March 12, 1960.

Borger, Julian. "It Came From Outer Toronto... Project Y: Secret Weapon 606A." *The Guardian*, Aug. 25, 1999.

Hadley, Ed. "U.S. Air Force Takes over Flying Saucer Project but Canada Likely to Share Results of Research." *Montreal Star*, Aug. 24, 1955.

Harrison, William C. "Aerial Oddballs: Strange Man-made Birds try their Wings under the California Sun." *AP News Feature*, Aug. 22, 1962.

"Retiring Designer Leaves Stamp on Aviation World." *The Daily News*, New Plymouth, New Zealand, May 22, 1979.

Robertson, Dalton. "Too Many Bugs Doomed the Canadian Avrocar." *Financial Post*, Sept. 23, 1961.

"Saucer Already Flying: Roe See New Era in Air." *Financial Post*, Oct. 31, 1959.

"Saucer Holds the Key to A. V. Roe's Future." *Financial Post*, April 18, 1959.

Williams, A.R. "Avro built a saucer-plane that actually flew." *Winnipeg Tribune*, TribFocus, Sat., Dec. 18, 1976.

AUDIO/VISUAL RESOURCES

AVROCAR. (VHS 20 min. B&W, Col.) Quadrent Video, Date unknown.

AVROCAR ... Avro's Flying Saucer. (VHS 25 min. B&W, Col.), Aviation Videos Limited, 1996.

Avro Arrow: CF-105... A Short History. (VHS 32 min. B&W, Col.), Burlington, A-V Studio, 1988.

The Arrow. CBC (four-hour mini-series), 1997.

The Arrow. (VHS 96 min. Col.) Norstar Entertainment, 1997.

Arrow: From Dream to Destruction. (VHS 60 min. B&W, Col.) Burlington, A-V Studio, 1992.

Front Page Challenge. (John Frost Interview) CBC, 1962.

Teskey, Susan, producer. *It Came from Malton.* The Fifth Estate, CBC, 1993.

The Wing Will Fly. A Discovery Channel Wings documentary on "Strange Planes."

UFO Coverups. In Search Of series episode.

ILLUSTRATIONS

Avrocar miscellaneous. B&W photos and photocopies of B&W photos.

Avrocar VZ-9-AV Assembly Breakdown & Details Complete Vehicle, Issue #1

Avrocar VZ-9-AV Assembly Breakdown and Details Common to Marry-Up of Lower Structure 1 N 530 Stage #1, Issue #1

Sketches of Avro (United Kingdom) 724 VTOL aircraft (alternative to Project Y)

VIRTUAL RESOURCES

De Pilonec, Marc. "Project Saucer. A collection of 233 documents researched by George Wright on the Avrocar." *Autodidactics*, P.O. Box 1549, La Jola, California, USA, 92038. 1998, (http://www.sdic.net/piolenc/saucer.htm).

Eldridge, Jason. " AVROLAND. A site dedicated to the people and aircraft of AVRO Canada & Orenda Engines Limited." 2001, (http://www.avroland.ca/al-vz9.html).

Mackechnie, David. "Avro Canada Archive on the Web. David Mackechnie's tribute to his father, Hugh Mackechnie, former Avro Canada photographer." 2000, (http://www.odyssey.on.ca/~dmackechnie)

McGrew, Charles. "Disc-shaped aircraft. An overview of projects based on unusual shapes for aircraft such as discs and wedges." 1999, (http://sloop.ee.fit.edu/users/lpinto/disc-sha.htm)

Saunders, Melvin D. "U.S. Manufactured Flying Saucers." © 1996 *Creative Alternatives - Home Page*, 2000, (http://www.tiac.net/users/seeker/creative.html).

Schmidt, R. Kyle. "Homage to the Avro Arrow." A reference source including a historical summary, illustrations and other links. 2000, (http://calum.csclub.uwaterloo.ca/u/rkschmid/Arrow/AvroArrow.html).

Zuk, Bill. "My Home Page. Excerpts from articles on Avro Canada and a link to the Bring Our Saucer Home Campaign." (http://www.autobahn.mb.ca/~billzuk/).

RELATED MATERIAL (TEXTUAL)

Air Force Releases Study on Unidentified Aerial Objects. USAF Fact Sheet 1053–55.

AVROCAR MARK II "Flying Saucer," info sheet. U.S. Army Transportation Museum, Fort Eustis, Virginia.

De Havilland DH.108 Swallow. Aircraft of the World Brochure, IMP Inc.,1988.

Review of AVRO GETOL/VTOL Future Development (Secret Session) given before the ad hoc committee on STOL/VTOL, Princeton University. Dec. 8–9, 1959.

U.S. Air Force contract file on the Avrocar. 1959–1961, USAF.

Welcome to the New Toronto Aerospace Museum brochure. 65 Carl Hall Road, Toronto, Ontario, M3K 2B6.

Wilkinson, Les, author. Notes and personal records made in 1980 and 1991.

INDEX

North American Air Defence (NORAD) 16, 18
North Atlantic Treaty Organization (NATO) 16–17, 89
North American Aviation 14, 16, 26, 80, 89
  F-86 Sabre 14, 16, 26
  P-51 (F-51) Mustang 26, 30
  XB-70 Valkyrie 80
  XF-108 Rapier 80
Northrop Aviation 32, 35, 38–40, 102
  B-2 Spirit 39
  MX-324 39
  N-1M 35, 39
  N-9M 39
  XB-35 Flying Wing 32, 38–39
  XB-49 and YB-49 Flying Wing 32, 38–39
  XP-56 39
  XP-79 Flying Ram 39
Northrop, Jack 32, 35, 38–40

Office of Naval Research (ONR) (US) 65
Ohain, Hans von 13
Operation Lusty 34
Operation Overcast 34
Operation Paperclip 34
Orrell, Jim 12
Ottawa, Canada 13, 17, 19, 20, 53, 86, 103

Panama Canal 74
Pearkes, George 23
Piasecki 64-65, 102
  59H Airgeep 65, 102
  59H Seageep 65
  59K 65
  VZ-8P(B) AirGeep II 65, 102
Poisson Aerospace 98
Potocki, Waldek ("Spud") 20, 76–77, 79, 87, 89
Powers, Jim 92
Pratt and Whitney J-75 19–20
Pratt and Whitney R-1830 33
Progressive Conservative Party of Canada 21
Project Blue Book 30–31
Project Grudge 30
Project Ladybird 55

Project Saucer (1948) 30
Project Sign 29–30
Project Silver Bug 57
Project Snowflake 97–98
Putt, Donald L. 54–56

Raeburn, Alex 44
Radcliffe, Geoffrey 91
Radio Corporation of America 19
RCA Victor Company 19
Ren TV 95–96
Rensselaer Polytechnic Institute 97
Reynolds-Alberta Museum 103
Rogers, Don 12
Rolls-Royce 14, 50, 51, 60
Rose, Arnold 9
Royal Air Force (RAF) 10, 47, 52
Royal Air Force Flying Review 47
Royal Canadian Air Force (RCAF) 7, 10, 12, 13–14, 17–19, 29, 31, 42, 47, 71
Royal Canadian Armoured Corps (RCAC) 88
Royal New Zealand Air Force (RNZAF) 91
Russia 46, 96
Rutkowski, Chris 98

Sack, Arthur 36
  AS-6 36
Saratov Aerospace Factory 96
  Ekip 96
Saunders Roe SRN1 84
  SRN2 84
  SRN5 84
Schauberger, Victor 34
Schriever, Rudolph 34
  Saucer 34
Scientific Advisory Board, (SAB) Office of the Chief of Staff, U.S. Government 54–55, 63
Sikorsky Aircraft 94–95
  Cypher 94–95
Silver Hills, Maryland 102
Slingsby Sailplanes 24
Smith, D.M. 47
Smye, Frederick 11, 17, 29
Soderburg, Dean 55

Solandt. Omond (Dr.) 44, 54
Special Projects Group 6, 7, 11, 24, 40, 42, 45, 67, 71–73, 81, 83, 85, 88, 98, 100
Straight Arrow Productions 100
Supermarine Spitfire 26
supersonic flight 18, 25–26, 28, 36, 44, 47–48, 54, 56–68, 60, 63, 66–69, 71–73, 80–82, 87, 89, 98

Takeuchi, Ray 40
Thorneycroft, Sir John Issac 83
Toronto, Ontario 8–10, 12, 29, 46–47, 53, 54, 100, 103
Toronto Aerospace Museum 53, 103
Toronto Star newspaper 46–47
Trans-Canada Air Lines (TCA) 12
Trans World Airlines (TWA) 13
Trudeau, Arthur G. 26, 64
Truman, Harry S. 39
Turbo Research 13–14

unidentified flying objects (UFO) 7, 29–31, 97–98
Union of Soviet Socialist Republics (USSR) (Soviet Union) *see* Russia 18, 21
United Kingdom 7, 10, 11, 12, 13, 24, 26, 29, 40, 42–43, 51–53, 84
United States Air Force (USAF) 29–32, 48, 53–57, 60, 62, 67–69, 71–72, 79–80, 96
United States Army (U.S. Army) 27, 34, 54, 64–69, 67–69, 71, 72, 80, 82, 95, 102–103
United States Army Air Force 38, 39
United States Army Transportation Museum 80, 82, 102–103
United States Army Transportation Research Command 65
United States Navy 30, 37, 49–50, 53, 56, 57, 65, 74, 96, 102
United States Navy Research Wind Tunnel *see* MIT 55, 57–58, 65
United States Pentagon 29, 57, 67, 69
unmanned aerial vehicles (UAV) 64, 94–95

V-2 34
Vandenberg, Hoyt S. 30
Verne, Jules 92
vectoring in forward flight (VIFF) 52
Victory Aircraft 10–13
Vought Aviation 32, 37–38
  V-173 32, 37–38
  XF5U-1 Flying Pancake 32, 37–38
VTOL 7, 21, 24, 35, 48–56, 59, 65, 67, 69, 71–72, 86–88, 92–94, 97–98, 101–103

Washington, D.C. 35, 69, 71, 80, 102–103
Waterton, Bill 28–29
Weapons Systems 606A (WS 606A) 53, 62–64, 67–69, 71–73, 78–83, 88, 96, 98, 100–101
Weiland, Carl 83
West Germany *see* Germany 31
Western Canada Aviation Museum 17, 49, 53, 103
Wetaskiwin, Alberta (Canada) 103
Wheelband, Al 40, 42, 47, 61, 71–72
White Sands Missile Range (WSMR), New Mexico 97
Whittle, Frank 13, 41
Whittley, Don 86
Williams International 95
  Wasp II 95
Williams Research Corporation 66–67
Williams, Ronald A. 29, 31, 46, 68–69, 77, 79, 83, 89
Wilkinson, Leslie "Les" 7–8, 11, 13, 29, 31, 55, 61, 85–89, 98, 100, 103
Winnipeg 8, 13, 100, 103
Winnipeg Tribune 17, 31, 46, 67
Wright-Patterson Air Force Base, Ohio 30, 57, 59, 96

Yeager, Charles E. "Chuck" 26

Zimmerman, Charles 37, 58
  "Zimmer Skimmer" 32, 36–37
Zurakowski, Janusz 8, 17–18, 20, 22, 28